THE AMAZING COLOMBIAN COOKBOOK

The Amazing Colombian Recipes

Camila Navia

Supernova Star Books

Copyright © 2023 Camila Navia

All rights reserved

No part of this book may be reproduced, or stored in a retrieval system, or transmitted in any form or by any means, electronic, mechanical, photocopying, recording, or otherwise, without express written permission of the publisher.

CONTENTS

Title Page
Copyright
Introduction
Appetizers   1
Salchichas envueltas   3
Deditos de queso   4
Arepas de choclo   6
Mini Tuna Patties   8
Arepas rellenas de pollo, aguacate y plátano maduro   9
Croquetas de atún (Tuna croquettes)   11
Montaditos (Small sandwiches)   13
Regañonas (Savory crackers)   14
Canastitas de atún (Tuna tartlets)   15
Ceviche de mango (Mango ceviche)   16
Abojarrados (Fried cassava and cheese balls)   17
Calloya (Fried plantains with cheese)   18
Ceviche de camarones (Shrimp ceviche)   19
Empanadas de jaiba (Crab empanadas)   20
Empanadas de pollo (Chicken empanadas)   22
Arepas vallunas (Valluna-style corn cakes)   24
Querrevengas (Colombian fried turnovers)   25

Papa rellena (Stuffed potato balls)	27
Tomatoes with spinach and ham (Tomates con espinaca y jamón)	28
Papas criollas rellenas de camarón (Creole-style shrimp-stuffed potatoes)	29
Breakfasts	31
Arepa with Grilled Beef	32
Arepa with Tuna and Shrimp	33
Carimañolas	34
Arepa de Huevo (Egg-stuffed arepa)	35
Huevos Pericos (Scrambled Eggs with Tomatoes and Onions)	37
Arepas de Queso (Cheese-stuffed arepas)	39
Chocolate in Coconut Milk	40
Calentado Colombiano (Colombian Breakfast Dish)	41
Arepas de Plátano Verde (Green Plantain Arepas)	42
Tortilla Paisa o Antioqueña (Antioquian-style Omelette)	43
Arepas con Pollo y Aguacate (Corn cakes with Chicken and Avocado)	44
Cayeye y Cabeza de Gato (Mashed Green Plantain and Pork Head)	45
Arepa con Carne Desmechada (Arepa with Shredded Beef)	46
Marranitas (Puerquitas)	47
Dips	49
Salsa de maní picante (Spicy peanut sauce)	50
Paté de cebolla y atún (Onion and tuna pate)	52
Salsa de mostaza (Mustard sauce)	53
Paté de jamón (Ham pâté)	54
Hogao (Colombian sauce made with onions, tomatoes, and	55

cilantro)

Manzana sauce	56
Salads	57
Ensalada de pulpo (Octopus salad)	58
Ensalada fría	59
Ensalada de aguacate y tomate (Avocado and Tomato Salad)	60
Ensalada de maíz y manzana (Corn and apple salad)	61
Vinagreta de aguacate (Avocado Vinaigrette)	62
Ensalada de lentejas y atún (Lentil and Tuna Salad)	63
Ensalada noche buena (Christmas Eve salad)	64
Ensalada de papa y atún (Potato and tuna salad)	65
Ensalada de queso y menta (Cheese and mint salad)	66
Ensalada Primaveral de Palmito (Spring Palm Heart Salad)	67
Soups	69
Cazuelitas de atún (Tuna casseroles)	70
Crema de zanahoria con jengibre (Carrot and ginger soup)	71
Cazuela de mariscos (Seafood casserole)	72
Crema de arveja (Pea Soup)	73
Sopa fría de aguacate (Cold Avocado Soup)	74
Ajíaco (Chicken and Potato Soup)	75
Crema de choclo (Cream of Corn Soup)	76
Mondongo (Tripe Soup)	77
Crema de champiñones (Cream of mushroom soup)	78
Sopa de guandú (Pigeon pea soup) recipe:	79
Shrimp soup	80
Crema de langosta, camarones o langostinos	81
Mute santandereano	82

Sopa de Manzana (Apple Soup)	83
Sopa de Tomate al Laurel (Tomato Soup with Bay Leaf)	84
Caldo de Queso y Cebollas (Cheese and Onion Soup)	85
Crema Campestre	86
Crema de calabaza y quinua con queso	87
Caldo de Guacuco	88
Sopa de almejas (Clam soup)	89
Mote de queso	90
Sancocho de cerdo salado	91
Caldo de Huevo (Egg soup)	92
Sancocho de Pato (Duck Sancocho)	93
Aborrajados de Pescado (Fried Plantain Stuffed with Fish)	94
Acorda de Langostinos (Shrimp Soup with Bread)	95
Main Dishes	97
Salpicón de Atún (Tuna Salad)	98
Arroz con Champiñones (Mushroom Rice)	99
Champiñones al Ajo (Garlic Mushrooms)	100
Chicharrones de Tocino (Bacon Cracklings)	101
Champiñones al ajo	102
Chicharrones de tocino	103
Colombinitas de pollo	104
Garbanzos a la mallorquina (Mallorcan-style chickpeas)	105
Rollitos de lechuga con pollo (Chicken lettuce wraps)	106
Camarones en apuro (Hurry-up shrimp)	107
Patacones con tomate	108
Pataconas desmechadas	109
Ceviche de quesos	110
Huevos con Bechamel	111

Pollo al Jengibre	112
Fricase de Pollo y Tocino (Chicken and Bacon Fricassee) from Colombia:	113
Crepes de pollo, champiñón y maní (Chicken, Mushroom, and Peanut Crepes):	115
Sobrebarriga en salsa	117
Picadillo	118
Lentejas a la criolla	119
Pipitoria de chivo	120
Bandeja paisa	122
Lomito de cerdo con salsa de papaya (Pork tenderloin with papaya sauce)	124
Macarrones con verduras (Macaroni with Vegetables):	125
Patacones especiales (Special Fried Plantains)	126
Salmón al whisky (Whiskey Salmon)	127
Patacones especiales (Special Fried Plantains)	128
Cerdo al curry con coco (Pork curry with coconut)	129
Arroz atollado de carne ahumada (Smoked meat rice stew)	130
Muchacho relleno colombiano	131
Lasaña de atún	133
Rollo de pollo navideño	134
Lentejas con chorizo	135
Lentejas con verduras	136
Tortillas de huevo con atún	137
Butifarra	138
Salmón con puré de papa criolla	139
Drinks and Beverages	141
Coctel de café	142

Salsa Coctel	143
Batido de mocka	144
Ponche Tropical	145
Avena	146
Caspiroleta	147
Crema de café colombiana	148
Agua de panela	149
Chicha	150
Masato	151
La macana	152
Fresco de aguacate	153
Chocolate con leche de coco (Coconut milk hot chocolate)	154
Café helado sorpresa (Surprise iced coffee)	155
Crema de café y chocolate (Coffee and chocolate cream)	156
Batido de banano al café (Banana and coffee smoothie)	157
Yogurt de chocolate (Chocolate yogurt)	158
Sorbete de fresa (Strawberry sorbet)	159
Crema de limón (Lemon cream):	160
Sorbete de chocolate y café (Chocolate and coffee sorbet)	161
Chocolate con leche de cocos (Chocolate with coconut milk)	162
Carajillo soul	163
Boxeador	164
Desserts	165
Alfajores colombianos	166
Buñuelos	167
Pastel de coco	168
Mantecada	169

Flan de café (Coffee Flan)	170
Postre borracho (Drunken dessert):	171
Bananos calados	172
Dulce de coco	173
Flan de queso	174
Arroz con leche	175
Mielmesabe	177
Flan de mango	178
Natilla	179
Trufas al café (coffee truffles)	180
Crepes al café (Coffee crepes)	181
Pastel de café (Coffee cake)	182
Bananos caramelizados con helado de vainilla	183
Cocadas Buenaventura	184
Mousse de Chocolate Blanco (White Chocolate Mousse)	185
Panna Cotta de Limonaria (Lemon Verbena Panna Cotta)	186
Torta de Auyama con Nibs de Cacao (Pumpkin Cake with Cacao Nibs)	188
Pan de Esponja (Sponge Bread)	189
Piononos	190
Merengón	192

INTRODUCTION

The Amazing Colombian Cookingbook is a celebration of the rich and diverse culinary heritage of Colombia. With 160 delicious recipes, it is a journey through the flavors, aromas, and colors that make Colombian cuisine so unique and fascinating.

Colombian food is the result of a blend of indigenous, European, and African influences, which have created a culinary tradition that is both flavorful and colorful. The native people of Colombia, such as the Muisca, Tayrona, and Quimbaya, relied heavily on corn, potatoes, and beans, which are still staples of the Colombian diet today. The Spanish brought with them ingredients such as pork, beef, rice, and wheat, while the Africans introduced tropical fruits, plantains, and spices.

The diversity of Colombia's geography has also played a significant role in shaping the country's cuisine. From the Andean region, where potatoes, quinoa, and corn are abundant, to the Caribbean coast, where seafood and coconut are the stars of the show, Colombian cuisine is as varied as the country itself.

The Amazing Colombian Cookingbook is a testament to this diversity, with recipes that range from hearty stews to light salads, from savory snacks to sweet desserts. You'll find classics such as Bandeja Paisa, Ajiaco, and Empanadas, as well as lesser-known gems like Lentejas con Verduras and Frijoles Antioqueños.

What sets Colombian cuisine apart is its use of fresh ingredients and bold flavors. Aji peppers, cilantro, cumin, and lime are just a few of the ingredients that give Colombian dishes their distinctive taste. And let's not forget about the national treasure that is Colombian coffee, which is used in desserts, drinks, and even savory dishes.

In conclusion, The Amazing Colombian Cookingbook is a tribute to the rich and diverse culinary heritage of Colombia, a country that is full of vibrant colors, bold flavors, and warm hospitality. Whether you're a seasoned cook or a beginner, this cookbook is sure to inspire you to explore the delicious world of Colombian cuisine.

APPETIZERS

SALCHICHAS ENVUELTAS

Ingredients:

8 hot dogs or sausages
8 slices of bacon
Toothpicks

Instructions:

Preheat oven to 375°F (190°C). Wrap each hot dog or sausage with a slice of bacon. Secure the bacon in place by inserting toothpicks at both ends of each sausage. Place the wrapped sausages on a baking sheet lined with parchment paper. Bake for 15-20 minutes or until the bacon is crispy and the sausages are cooked through.

Serve hot and enjoy!

DEDITOS DE QUESO

Ingredients:

8-10 mozzarella cheese sticks
1 cup all-purpose flour
2 eggs
1 cup breadcrumbs
Vegetable oil, for frying

Instructions:

Cut the cheese sticks into bite-size pieces. Place the flour, beaten eggs, and breadcrumbs into three separate bowls. Roll each piece of cheese in the flour, then dip into the egg, and finally coat with breadcrumbs. Heat vegetable oil in a deep frying pan over medium-high heat. Fry the cheese sticks in batches for 1-2 minutes or until golden brown. Drain on paper towels and serve hot with your favorite dipping sauce.

AREPAS DE CHOCLO

Ingredients:

2 cups sweet corn kernels
1 cup masarepa (pre-cooked cornmeal)
1 cup warm water
1/2 tsp salt
1/4 cup vegetable oil

Instructions:

In a blender or food processor, blend the corn kernels until smooth. In a large mixing bowl, combine the corn puree, masarepa, warm water, and salt. Mix until well combined. Let the mixture rest for 5-10 minutes to allow the masarepa to absorb the water.
Form the dough into 8-10 small patties, about 1/2 inch

thick. Heat vegetable oil in a non-stick pan over medium heat. Cook the arepas for about 5-7 minutes on each side or until golden brown and crispy. Serve hot with your favorite toppings such as cheese, avocado, or tomato sauce. Enjoy!

MINI TUNA PATTIES

Ingredients:

2 cans of tuna, drained
1/4 cup finely chopped onion
1/4 cup finely chopped red bell pepper
1/4 cup finely chopped green bell pepper
1/4 cup mayonnaise
1/4 cup breadcrumbs
1 egg
1/2 tsp salt
1/4 tsp black pepper
Vegetable oil, for frying

Instructions:

In a large mixing bowl, combine the drained tuna, chopped onion, red and green bell pepper, mayonnaise, breadcrumbs, egg, salt, and black pepper. Mix well. Form the mixture into small patties, about 2-3 inches in diameter. Heat vegetable oil in a frying pan over medium-high heat. Fry the mini tuna patties in batches for 2-3 minutes or until golden brown and crispy. Drain on paper towels and serve hot with your favorite dipping sauce.

AREPAS RELLENAS DE POLLO, AGUACATE Y PLÁTANO MADURO

(Corn cakes stuffed with chicken, avocado, and ripe plantain)

Ingredients:

2 cups of precooked cornmeal (masa)
2 cups of warm water
1 teaspoon of salt
2 tablespoons of vegetable oil
2 cups of shredded cooked chicken
1 ripe plantain, mashed
1 ripe avocado, mashed
1 small onion, finely chopped
2 garlic cloves, minced
1 tablespoon of vegetable oil
Salt and pepper to taste

Instructions:

In a bowl, mix the precooked cornmeal, warm water, salt, and vegetable oil until you obtain a soft dough. Let it rest for 10 minutes. In a pan, heat the vegetable oil over medium heat. Add the onion and garlic and sauté until the onion is translucent. Add the shredded chicken, mashed plantain, mashed avocado, salt, and pepper. Stir well and cook for 5 minutes. Divide the corn dough into 8 equal portions and shape them into balls. Flatten each ball with your hands to form a disk. Put a spoonful of the chicken and plantain mixture in the center of each disk.
Fold the edges of the dough over the filling to form a ball.
Heat a non-stick skillet over medium heat. Cook the arepas for

5-7 minutes on each side, or until golden brown and cooked through.

Serve hot and enjoy!

CROQUETAS DE ATÚN
(TUNA CROQUETTES)

Ingredients:

2 cans of tuna in water, drained
2 tablespoons of butter
2 tablespoons of all-purpose flour
1 cup of milk
1/4 teaspoon of salt
1/4 teaspoon of black pepper
1/4 teaspoon of garlic powder
1/4 teaspoon of onion powder
1/4 teaspoon of dried oregano
1/4 teaspoon of dried thyme
1/4 cup of bread crumbs
1 egg, beaten
Vegetable oil for frying

Instructions:

In a pan, melt the butter over medium heat. Add the flour and whisk until smooth. Gradually add the milk, stirring constantly until the mixture thickens. Add the tuna, salt, black pepper, garlic powder, onion powder, oregano, and thyme. Stir until well combined. Transfer the mixture to a bowl and let it cool for 30 minutes. With your hands, shape the mixture into small croquettes. Dip each croquette into the beaten egg, then coat with bread crumbs.
Heat the vegetable oil in a deep-fryer or a pan over medium heat. Fry the croquettes until golden brown.Drain on paper towels and serve hot.

MONTADITOS (SMALL SANDWICHES)

Ingredients:

Baguette or any type of bread you prefer, sliced
1 tomato, sliced
1 small onion, sliced
1 avocado, sliced
4 slices of ham
4 slices of cheese
Mayonnaise
Salt and pepper to taste

Instructions:

Toast the bread slices. Spread mayonnaise on each slice. Layer the tomato, onion, avocado, ham, and cheese on top of each slice. Sprinkle with salt and pepper to taste. Serve cold.

REGAÑONAS (SAVORY CRACKERS)

Ingredients:

2 cups all-purpose flour
1/2 cup unsalted butter, softened
1/4 cup water
1 tsp salt
1 tsp paprika
1 tsp garlic powder
1 tsp onion powder
1 tsp dried oregano
1/2 tsp baking powder

Instructions:

In a large mixing bowl, combine the flour, salt, paprika, garlic powder, onion powder, dried oregano, and baking powder. Mix well. Add the softened butter and mix until the mixture resembles coarse crumbs. Gradually add the water and mix until the dough comes together. Divide the dough into 2 equal portions and shape each into a disc. Wrap in plastic wrap and refrigerate for at least 30 minutes. Preheat the oven to 375°F (190°C). Line a baking sheet with parchment paper. On a lightly floured surface, roll out one disc of dough to 1/8 inch thickness. Cut the dough into small rectangles using a sharp knife or pizza cutter. Transfer the crackers onto the prepared baking sheet. Bake for 10-12 minutes, or until lightly golden brown. Allow the crackers to cool on the baking sheet for 5 minutes before transferring to a wire rack to cool completely. Repeat with the remaining dough.

CANASTITAS DE ATÚN (TUNA TARTLETS)

Ingredients:

1 can of tuna, drained
1/4 cup mayonnaise
1/4 cup diced red onion
2 tbsp diced celery
2 tbsp diced red bell pepper
1 tbsp lemon juice
1/2 tsp salt
1/4 tsp black pepper
12 mini tart shells

Instructions:

Preheat the oven to 350°F (175°C). In a mixing bowl, combine the tuna, mayonnaise, red onion, celery, red bell pepper, lemon juice, salt, and black pepper. Mix well. Fill each tart shell with the tuna mixture. Place the tartlets on a baking sheet and bake for 10-12 minutes, or until the tart shells are golden brown. Serve warm.

CEVICHE DE MANGO (MANGO CEVICHE)

Ingredients:

2 ripe mangoes, peeled and diced
1/2 red onion, finely chopped
1/4 cup chopped fresh cilantro
1 jalapeño pepper, seeded and finely chopped
2 limes, juiced
Salt and black pepper, to taste

Instructions:

In a mixing bowl, combine the diced mango, red onion, cilantro, and jalapeño pepper. Add the lime juice and season with salt and black pepper to taste. Mix well. Cover and refrigerate for at least 30 minutes. Serve chilled.

ABOJARRADOS (FRIED CASSAVA AND CHEESE BALLS)

Ingredients:

2 cups cassava, cooked and mashed
1 cup queso blanco (white cheese), crumbled
1 egg
Salt to taste
Oil for frying

Instructions:

In a large mixing bowl, combine the mashed cassava, crumbled queso blanco, and salt. Mix well. Add the egg to the mixture and continue mixing until everything is well combined. Using your hands, form the mixture into small balls. Heat oil in a frying pan over medium-high heat. Once hot, carefully place the cassava balls in the pan, making sure not to overcrowd them. Fry the cassava balls until golden brown on all sides. Remove from the pan and place on paper towels to absorb excess oil. Serve hot as an appetizer or snack.

CALLOYA (FRIED PLANTAINS WITH CHEESE)

Ingredients:

4 ripe plantains
1 cup queso blanco (white cheese), crumbled
Oil for frying

Instructions:

Peel the plantains and cut them into 1-inch slices. Heat oil in a frying pan over medium-high heat. Once hot, carefully place the plantain slices in the pan, making sure not to overcrowd them. Fry the plantain slices until golden brown on both sides. Remove from the pan and place on paper towels to absorb excess oil. While the plantains are still hot, sprinkle them with the crumbled queso blanco. Serve hot as an appetizer or side dish. I hope you enjoy these recipes!

CEVICHE DE CAMARONES (SHRIMP CEVICHE)

Ingredients:

1 lb medium-sized shrimp, peeled and deveined
1/2 red onion, finely chopped
1 red bell pepper, diced
1 yellow bell pepper, diced
1 green bell pepper, diced
1/2 cup lime juice
1/4 cup orange juice
Salt and pepper to taste
Cilantro, chopped
1 avocado, diced

Instructions:

In a large mixing bowl, combine the shrimp, red onion, bell peppers, lime juice, orange juice, salt, and pepper. Mix well. Cover and refrigerate for at least 30 minutes, or until the shrimp is cooked through. Garnish with chopped cilantro and diced avocado before serving.

EMPANADAS DE JAIBA (CRAB EMPANADAS)

Ingredients:

2 cups flour
1/4 cup butter, chilled and diced
1/4 cup vegetable shortening, chilled and diced
1/4 cup water
1/4 cup white wine
1/4 tsp salt
1/4 tsp sugar
1 egg, beaten
1 lb crab meat, cooked and shredded
1/2 red bell pepper, diced
1/2 yellow onion, diced
2 tbsp vegetable oil

Salt and pepper to taste

Instructions:
In a large mixing bowl, combine the flour, chilled butter, chilled shortening, water, white wine, salt, and sugar. Mix until the dough comes together. Wrap the dough in plastic wrap and refrigerate for 30 minutes. In a skillet, heat the vegetable oil over medium heat. Add the red bell pepper and onion and sauté until softened. Add the cooked crab meat, salt, and pepper. Mix well and cook for 2-3 minutes. Preheat the oven to 375°F (190°C). Roll out the chilled dough and cut out circles using a cookie cutter. Spoon the crab mixture onto each dough circle and fold in half. Use a fork to press the edges together and seal. Brush each empanada with beaten egg and bake for 20-25 minutes, or until golden brown.
Serve warm.

EMPANADAS DE POLLO (CHICKEN EMPANADAS)

Ingredients:
2 cups all-purpose flour
1/2 teaspoon salt
1/4 cup cold unsalted butter, cut into small cubes
1/4 cup cold water
1 egg, beaten
1 tablespoon olive oil
1 small onion, chopped
1 garlic clove, minced
2 cups cooked and shredded chicken
1/4 cup chopped green olives
1/4 cup raisins
Salt and pepper, to taste
Oil, for frying

Instructions:

In a large bowl, mix the flour and salt together. Add the butter and use your fingers to rub it into the flour mixture until it resembles coarse crumbs. Add the water and mix until the dough comes together. Cover and refrigerate for at least 30 minutes. In a skillet over medium heat, heat the olive oil. Add the onion and garlic and cook until the onion is soft and translucent. Add the chicken, olives, raisins, salt, and pepper. Cook for 5 minutes, stirring occasionally. Set aside to cool. Roll out the dough on a lightly floured surface and cut out circles using a cookie cutter or a glass. Place a tablespoon of the chicken mixture on each dough circle. Fold the dough over to enclose the filling and seal the edges by pressing with a fork. In a large skillet over medium-high heat, heat the oil. Fry the empanadas until golden brown on both sides. Drain on paper towels and serve hot.

AREPAS VALLUNAS (VALLUNA-STYLE CORN CAKES)

Ingredients:

2 cups precooked cornmeal (masarepa)
1 teaspoon salt
2 cups warm water
1/2 cup cooked and shredded chicken
1/2 cup cooked and shredded pork
1/4 cup hogao (Colombian sauce made with onions, tomatoes, and cilantro)
1/4 cup grated queso blanco
Oil, for frying

Instructions:

In a large bowl, mix the cornmeal and salt together. Add the warm water and mix well until the dough comes together. Divide the dough into 8 equal pieces and shape them into disks. In a skillet over medium-high heat, heat a little bit of oil. Cook the arepas for 3-4 minutes on each side or until golden brown. In a bowl, mix the chicken, pork, and hogao together. Season with salt and pepper to taste. Cut each arepa in half and fill with the chicken and pork mixture. Top with grated queso blanco. Serve hot and enjoy!

QUERREVENGAS (COLOMBIAN FRIED TURNOVERS)

Ingredients:

For the dough:

2 cups all-purpose flour
1 teaspoon baking powder
1 teaspoon salt
1/2 cup water
1/2 cup vegetable shortening

For the filling:

1 pound ground beef
1 onion, finely chopped
1 red bell pepper, finely chopped
2 garlic cloves, minced
2 tablespoons tomato paste
1 teaspoon ground cumin
1/2 teaspoon dried oregano
1/2 cup beef broth
Salt and pepper, to taste
Oil, for frying

Instructions:

To make the dough, in a large bowl, mix together the flour, baking powder, and salt. Add the water and vegetable shortening and mix until a dough forms. Knead for a few minutes until the dough is smooth and elastic. To make the filling, heat a little bit of oil in a skillet over medium-high heat. Add the ground beef and cook, breaking it up with a wooden spoon, until browned. Add the onion, bell pepper, garlic, tomato paste, cumin, and oregano and cook for a few more minutes. Add the beef broth and simmer until most of the liquid has evaporated. Season with salt and pepper to taste. To assemble the turnovers, divide the dough into 12 equal pieces and roll each piece into a ball. Flatten each ball with a rolling pin and place a spoonful of the filling in the center. Fold the dough over the filling to form a half-moon shape and seal the edges with a fork. Heat oil in a large skillet over medium-high heat. Fry the turnovers, a few at a time, until golden brown on both sides. Drain on paper towels.

PAPA RELLENA (STUFFED POTATO BALLS)

Ingredients:

6 large potatoes, peeled and cubed
1 tablespoon vegetable oil
1 onion, finely chopped
2 garlic cloves, minced
1 pound ground beef
1 teaspoon ground cumin
1/2 teaspoon dried oregano
Salt and pepper, to taste
1 egg, lightly beaten
1 cup all-purpose flour
Oil, for frying

Instructions:

In a large pot, cook the potatoes in salted water until tender. Drain and mash the potatoes. In a large skillet, heat the oil over medium-high heat. Add the onion and garlic and cook until soft. Add the ground beef and cook, breaking it up with a wooden spoon, until browned. Add the cumin, oregano, salt, and pepper and cook for a few more minutes. Remove from the heat and let cool. To assemble the stuffed potato balls, take a handful of mashed potatoes and shape it into a ball. Make a well in the center and fill it with a spoonful of the beef mixture. Close the potato ball around the filling and shape it into a round ball. Dip each potato ball in the beaten egg and then coat with flour. Heat oil in a large skillet over medium-high heat. Fry the potato balls until golden brown on all sides. Drain on paper towels.

TOMATOES WITH SPINACH AND HAM (TOMATES CON ESPINACA Y JAMÓN)

Ingredients:

4 medium tomatoes
1/2 cup cooked spinach, chopped
1/2 cup cooked ham, diced
1/2 cup grated Parmesan cheese
1/4 cup bread crumbs
1 tablespoon olive oil
Salt and pepper to taste

Instructions:

Preheat oven to 375°F (190°C). Cut off the tops of the tomatoes and scoop out the pulp and seeds, leaving a shell.

In a bowl, mix the spinach, ham, Parmesan cheese, bread crumbs, olive oil, salt, and pepper together. Stuff the tomato shells with the mixture and place them in a baking dish. Bake for 20-25 minutes or until the tomatoes are tender and the filling is golden brown.

PAPAS CRIOLLAS RELLENAS DE CAMARÓN (CREOLE-STYLE SHRIMP-STUFFED POTATOES)

Ingredients:

4 large potatoes
1 pound cooked shrimp, peeled and deveined
1/2 cup chopped onion
1/2 cup chopped tomato
1/4 cup chopped cilantro
1/4 cup mayonnaise
1 tablespoon lime juice
Salt and pepper to taste

Instructions:

Preheat oven to 375°F (190°C). Wash and scrub the potatoes. Pierce them with a fork and bake for 45-60 minutes or until tender. Cut off the tops of the potatoes and scoop out the flesh, leaving a shell. In a bowl, mix the shrimp, onion, tomato, cilantro, mayonnaise, lime juice, salt, and pepper together. Stuff the potato shells with the mixture and place them in a baking dish. Bake for 15-20 minutes or until the filling is heated through and the potatoes are golden brown.

BREAKFASTS

AREPA WITH GRILLED BEEF

Ingredients:

2 cups precooked cornmeal (masarepa)
1 teaspoon salt
2 cups warm water
1 lb grilled beef, sliced
1 avocado, sliced
1/4 cup grated queso blanco
Oil, for frying

Instructions:

In a large bowl, mix the cornmeal and salt together. Add the warm water and mix well until the dough comes together. Divide the dough into 8 equal pieces and shape them into disks. In a skillet over medium-high heat, heat a little bit of oil. Cook the arepas for 3-4 minutes on each side or until golden brown. Cut the arepas in half and fill them with the grilled beef, avocado, and grated queso blanco.

AREPA WITH TUNA AND SHRIMP

Ingredients:

2 cups precooked cornmeal (masarepa)
1 teaspoon salt
2 cups warm water
1 can tuna, drained
1/2 lb cooked shrimp, peeled and deveined
1/4 cup mayonnaise
1/4 cup chopped fresh cilantro
Oil, for frying

Instructions:

In a large bowl, mix the cornmeal and salt together. Add the warm water and mix well until the dough comes together. Divide the dough into 8 equal pieces and shape them into disks. In a skillet over medium-high heat, heat a little bit of oil. Cook the arepas for 3-4 minutes on each side or until golden brown. In a bowl, mix the tuna, cooked shrimp, mayonnaise, and cilantro together. Season with salt and pepper to taste. Cut the arepas in half and fill them with the tuna and shrimp mixture.

CARIMAÑOLAS

Ingredients:

2 cups mashed yuca
1/2 lb ground beef
1/4 cup chopped onion
1/4 cup chopped green bell pepper
1/4 cup chopped tomato
1/4 cup chopped cilantro
2 cloves garlic, minced
1/2 tsp ground cumin
Salt and pepper, to taste
Oil, for frying

Instructions:

In a skillet over medium-high heat, cook the ground beef until browned. Add the onion, green bell pepper, tomato, cilantro, garlic, cumin, salt, and pepper. Cook until the vegetables are tender. In a bowl, mix the mashed yuca with a little bit of salt. Take a golf ball-sized amount of the yuca mixture and shape it into a small cylinder. Make a hole in the center and fill it with a spoonful of the beef mixture. Close the hole and shape the yuca mixture into a small football shape. In a deep skillet or fryer, heat the oil to 350°F. Fry the carimañolas until golden brown, about 5-6 minutes. Drain on paper towels before serving.

AREPA DE HUEVO (EGG-STUFFED AREPA)

Ingredients:

2 cups of arepa flour
2 and 1/2 cups of warm water
1 teaspoon of salt
4 eggs
1/2 cup of vegetable oil

Instructions:

In a bowl, mix the arepa flour, salt and warm water until the dough is smooth and uniform. Make 4 dough balls and flatten them to form disks. In a skillet over medium-high heat, add a little bit of oil and cook the arepas for about 5 minutes on each side, until they are golden brown. Remove the arepas from the skillet and set them aside. In a separate skillet, scramble the eggs and set them aside. Cut a small hole in the middle of each arepa and stuff them with the scrambled eggs. Serve hot.

HUEVOS PERICOS (SCRAMBLED EGGS WITH TOMATOES AND ONIONS)

Ingredients:

4 eggs
1 small onion, finely chopped
2 small tomatoes, finely chopped
1 tablespoon of vegetable oil
Salt and pepper to taste

Instructions:

In a skillet over medium heat, heat the oil and sauté the onions until they are soft and translucent. Add the tomatoes and cook for about 3 minutes, until they are soft. In a separate bowl, beat the eggs and add them to the skillet.

Stir the mixture occasionally until the eggs are cooked through. Season with salt and pepper to taste. Serve hot with arepas or bread.

AREPA CON CARNE DESMECHADA (AREPA WITH SHREDDED BEEF)

Ingredients:

2 cups precooked white cornmeal (masarepa)
2 1/2 cups warm water
1 teaspoon salt
1 pound beef brisket, cooked and shredded
1/2 onion, chopped
1/2 red bell pepper, chopped
1/2 green bell pepper, chopped
2 cloves garlic, minced
2 tablespoons vegetable oil
Salt and pepper, to taste

Instructions:

In a large bowl, mix the cornmeal, salt, and warm water until a dough forms. Divide the dough into 8 equal pieces and shape them into disks. Heat a griddle or non-stick pan over medium heat. Cook the arepas for about 5 minutes on each side or until golden brown. In a skillet, heat the oil over medium-high heat. Add the onion, bell peppers, and garlic and sauté for about 3-4 minutes or until tender. Add the shredded beef and cook for another 3-4 minutes or until heated through. Season with salt and pepper to taste.
Slice the arepas in half and stuff them with the beef mixture. Serve warm.

CAYEYE Y CABEZA DE GATO (MASHED GREEN PLANTAIN AND PORK HEAD)

Ingredients:

4 green plantains, peeled and chopped
2 cups water
1/2 pound pork head, cooked and diced
1/2 cup diced scallions
Salt and pepper, to taste
Oil, for frying

Instructions:

In a pot, bring the chopped plantains and water to a boil. Reduce heat and simmer for 10-15 minutes or until the plantains are soft. Drain the water and mash the plantains with a fork or potato masher. In a skillet over medium-high heat, heat a little bit of oil. Add the diced pork head and cook for 3-4 minutes or until golden brown. Add the scallions and cook for an additional 1-2 minutes.
Season the mashed plantains with salt and pepper to taste. Serve the mashed plantains with the pork head mixture on top.

AREPAS CON POLLO Y AGUACATE (CORN CAKES WITH CHICKEN AND AVOCADO)

Ingredients:

2 cups precooked cornmeal (masarepa)
1 teaspoon salt
2 cups warm water
1/2 cup cooked and shredded chicken
1 avocado, diced
Salt and pepper, to taste
Oil, for frying

Instructions:

In a large bowl, mix the cornmeal and salt together. Add the warm water and mix well until the dough comes together. Divide the dough into 8 equal pieces and shape them into disks. In a skillet over medium-high heat, heat a little bit of oil. Cook the arepas for 3-4 minutes on each side or until golden brown. In a bowl, mix the chicken and diced avocado together. Season with salt and pepper to taste. Slice the arepas in half and stuff them with the chicken and avocado mixture. Serve warm.

TORTILLA PAISA O ANTIOQUEÑA (ANTIOQUIAN-STYLE OMELETTE)

Ingredients:
4 eggs
1/2 cup cooked and diced potatoes
1/2 cup cooked and diced pork belly
1/2 cup cooked and diced chorizo sausage
1/2 cup diced scallions
Salt and pepper, to taste
Oil, for frying

Instructions:

In a bowl, whisk the eggs with a little bit of salt and pepper. In a skillet over medium-high heat, heat a little bit of oil. Add the potatoes, pork belly, and chorizo and cook for 3-4 minutes or until golden brown. Add the scallions and cook for an additional 1-2 minutes. Pour the whisked eggs into the skillet and cook until the bottom is set. Using a spatula, flip the omelette over and cook for an additional 1-2 minutes or until cooked through. Serve hot.

AREPAS DE PLÁTANO VERDE (GREEN PLANTAIN AREPAS)

Ingredients:

2 green plantains, peeled and cut into chunks
1/4 cup pre-cooked cornmeal (masarepa)
1/2 cup grated mozzarella cheese
Salt, to taste
Oil, for frying

Instructions:

In a food processor, pulse the green plantain chunks until they are finely ground. Transfer the ground plantain to a large bowl and mix in the pre-cooked cornmeal and salt until well combined. Stir in the grated mozzarella cheese until well distributed. Divide the mixture into 6-8 equal portions and shape them into flat disks. In a large skillet or griddle, heat a little bit of oil over medium-high heat. Cook the arepas for 3-4 minutes on each side, until golden brown and crispy. Serve hot with your favorite toppings or fillings.

CALENTADO COLOMBIANO (COLOMBIAN BREAKFAST DISH)

Ingredients:

2 cups leftover cooked rice
1 cup cooked red beans
1/2 cup chopped cooked pork belly or bacon
1/2 cup chopped cooked sausage
1/4 cup chopped green onion
Salt and pepper, to taste
2 tablespoons vegetable oil

Instructions:

In a large skillet or wok, heat the vegetable oil over medium heat. Add the cooked rice, red beans, chopped pork belly or bacon, and sausage to the skillet and stir to combine. Cook the mixture for 10-15 minutes, stirring occasionally, until everything is heated through and the rice is slightly crispy. Season the mixture with salt and pepper to taste. Serve hot and garnish with chopped green onion.

CHOCOLATE IN COCONUT MILK

Ingredients:

2 cups coconut milk
1/2 cup dark chocolate chips
1/4 cup honey
1/4 teaspoon ground cinnamon
Pinch of salt

Instructions:

In a medium-sized saucepan, heat the coconut milk over medium heat until it starts to simmer. Add the dark chocolate chips, honey, cinnamon, and salt to the saucepan and whisk continuously until the chocolate has melted and the mixture is smooth.Let the mixture simmer for another 3-5 minutes, whisking occasionally.Serve hot in mugs and enjoy!

AREPAS DE QUESO (CHEESE-STUFFED AREPAS)

Ingredients:

2 cups of arepa flour
2 and 1/2 cups of warm water
1 teaspoon of salt
1 cup of grated cheese (such as queso blanco or mozzarella)
1/2 cup of vegetable oil

Instructions:

In a bowl, mix the arepa flour, salt and warm water until the dough is smooth and uniform. Make 8 dough balls and flatten them to form disks. Add a tablespoon of grated cheese to the center of each disk and fold them in half. Use your fingers to seal the edges of the arepas. In a skillet over medium-high heat, add a little bit of oil and cook the arepas for about 5 minutes on each side, until they are golden brown. Remove the arepas from the skillet and set them aside. Serve hot.

MARRANITAS (PUERQUITAS)

Ingredients:

2 ripe plantains, peeled and mashed
1/2 cup pork rinds, crushed
1/4 cup all-purpose flour
1/4 cup finely chopped onion
2 tablespoons finely chopped cilantro
Salt and pepper, to taste
Oil, for frying

Instructions:

In a large bowl, mix the mashed plantains, pork rinds, flour, onion, and cilantro until well combined. Season with salt and pepper to taste. Heat about 1 inch of oil in a heavy-bottomed skillet or pot over medium-high heat. Using a spoon, drop the plantain mixture into the hot oil, forming small patties. Fry the patties for about 2-3 minutes on each side or until golden brown. Using a slotted spoon, transfer the marranitas to a plate lined with paper towels to drain excess oil. Serve warm.

DIPS

SALSA DE MANÍ PICANTE (SPICY PEANUT SAUCE)

Ingredients:

1/2 cup peanut butter
1/4 cup soy sauce
2 tablespoons rice vinegar
1 tablespoon brown sugar
1 teaspoon Sriracha sauce
1/4 teaspoon garlic powder
1/4 teaspoon ground ginger
1/4 cup water

Instructions:

In a mixing bowl, whisk together the peanut butter, soy sauce, rice vinegar, brown sugar, Sriracha sauce, garlic powder, and ground ginger. Gradually add the water, whisking until smooth. Taste and adjust seasonings as needed. Serve as a dipping sauce or drizzle over stir-fry dishes.

PATÉ DE CEBOLLA Y ATÚN (ONION AND TUNA PATE)

Ingredients:

1 can tuna, drained
1/4 cup mayonnaise
1/4 cup sour cream
1/2 cup chopped onion
1 tablespoon lemon juice
Salt and pepper to taste
Crackers or bread, for serving

Instructions:

In a mixing bowl, combine the drained tuna, mayonnaise, and sour cream. Add the chopped onion and lemon juice. Season with salt and pepper to taste. Mix well and chill for at least 1 hour. Serve with crackers or bread.

SALSA DE MOSTAZA (MUSTARD SAUCE)

Ingredients:

1/2 cup mayonnaise
1/4 cup Dijon mustard
1 tablespoon honey
1 tablespoon apple cider vinegar
Salt and black pepper, to taste

Instructions:

In a small bowl, whisk together the mayonnaise, Dijon mustard, honey, and apple cider vinegar. Season with salt and black pepper to taste. Serve as a dipping sauce or spread for sandwiches.

PATÉ DE JAMÓN (HAM PÂTÉ)

Ingredients:

1 pound cooked ham, chopped
1/2 cup cream cheese, softened
1/4 cup mayonnaise
1 tablespoon Dijon mustard
2 tablespoons chopped fresh parsley
Salt and black pepper, to taste

Instructions:

In a food processor, combine the chopped ham, cream cheese, mayonnaise, and Dijon mustard. Pulse until well blended and smooth. Add the chopped parsley and pulse a few times to combine. Season with salt and black pepper to taste. Serve as a spread for crackers or bread.

HOGAO (COLOMBIAN SAUCE MADE WITH ONIONS, TOMATOES, AND CILANTRO)

Ingredients:

2 tablespoons vegetable oil
1 large onion, chopped
3 large tomatoes, chopped
1/4 cup chopped fresh cilantro
Salt and black pepper, to taste

Instructions:

In a large skillet, heat the vegetable oil over medium heat. Add the chopped onion and cook until softened and translucent, about 5-7 minutes. Add the chopped tomatoes and cook for another 5-7 minutes, or until the tomatoes have broken down and the mixture is thick and saucy. Stir in the chopped cilantro and season with salt and black pepper to taste. Serve as a condiment for meats, rice, or beans.

MANZANA SAUCE

Ingredients:

2 large apples, peeled and grated
1/2 cup mayonnaise
1/2 cup sour cream
2 tablespoons honey
1/4 teaspoon ground cinnamon

Instructions:

In a bowl, mix together the grated apples, mayonnaise, sour cream, honey, and cinnamon. Cover the bowl and refrigerate for at least 30 minutes to allow the flavors to blend. Serve the dip with sliced fruit, crackers, or toasted bread. I hope this recipe is more helpful. Let me know if you have any further questions!

SALADS

ENSALADA DE PULPO (OCTOPUS SALAD)

Ingredients:

1 lb octopus, cooked and diced
2 tomatoes, diced
1 red onion, thinly sliced
1 green bell pepper, diced
1 red bell pepper, diced
1/4 cup cilantro, chopped
1/4 cup lime juice
1/4 cup olive oil
Salt and pepper to taste

Instructions:

In a large bowl, mix together the octopus, tomatoes, onion, bell peppers, and cilantro. In a separate bowl, whisk together the lime juice, olive oil, salt, and pepper. Pour the dressing over the salad and toss to coat. Chill in the refrigerator for at least 30 minutes before serving.

ENSALADA FRÍA

Ingredients:

2 cups cooked rice
1 can of corn, drained
1 can of peas, drained
1 can of carrots, drained and diced
1 red bell pepper, diced
1/4 cup chopped parsley
1/4 cup mayonnaise
1/4 cup sour cream
1/4 cup milk
Salt and pepper to taste

Instructions:

In a large bowl, mix together the rice, corn, peas, carrots, red bell pepper, and parsley. In a separate bowl, whisk together the mayonnaise, sour cream, milk, salt, and pepper. Pour the dressing over the salad and toss to coat. Chill in the refrigerator for at least 30 minutes before serving.

ENSALADA DE AGUACATE Y TOMATE (AVOCADO AND TOMATO SALAD)

Ingredients:

2 ripe avocados, diced
2 ripe tomatoes, diced
1 small red onion, sliced
1/4 cup fresh cilantro, chopped
1 lime, juiced
2 tablespoons olive oil
Salt and pepper, to taste

Instructions:

In a large bowl, combine the diced avocados, tomatoes, sliced red onion, and chopped cilantro. In a separate small bowl, whisk together the lime juice, olive oil, salt, and pepper to make the dressing. Pour the dressing over the salad and toss gently to combine. Serve chilled or at room temperature.

ENSALADA DE MAÍZ Y MANZANA (CORN AND APPLE SALAD)

Ingredients:

2 cups cooked corn
1 apple, diced
1 red onion, diced
1/4 cup chopped cilantro
1/4 cup lime juice
1/4 cup olive oil
Salt and pepper to taste

Instructions:

In a large bowl, mix together the corn, apple, onion, and cilantro. In a separate bowl, whisk together the lime juice, olive oil, salt, and pepper. Pour the dressing over the salad and toss to coat. Chill in the refrigerator for at least 30 minutes before serving.

VINAGRETA DE AGUACATE (AVOCADO VINAIGRETTE)

Ingredients:

1 ripe avocado
1/4 cup white vinegar
1/4 cup olive oil
1 garlic clove, minced
1 teaspoon honey
Salt and pepper, to taste

Instructions:

In a blender or food processor, combine the ripe avocado, white vinegar, olive oil, minced garlic, and honey. Blend until the mixture is smooth and creamy. Season with salt and pepper to taste. Drizzle the vinaigrette over your favorite salad and enjoy!

ENSALADA DE LENTEJAS Y ATÚN (LENTIL AND TUNA SALAD)

Ingredients:

2 cups cooked lentils
2 cans of tuna, drained
1 red bell pepper, diced
1/2 red onion, diced
1/4 cup fresh parsley, chopped
1/4 cup fresh cilantro, chopped
1 lime, juiced
2 tablespoons olive oil
Salt and pepper, to taste

Instructions:

In a large bowl, combine the cooked lentils, drained tuna, diced red bell pepper, diced red onion, chopped parsley, and chopped cilantro. In a separate small bowl, whisk together the lime juice, olive oil, salt, and pepper to make the dressing. Pour the dressing over the salad and toss gently to combine. Serve chilled or at room temperature.

ENSALADA NOCHE BUENA (CHRISTMAS EVE SALAD)

Ingredients:

1 lb potatoes, peeled and cubed
1 lb carrots, peeled and sliced
1 can of peas, drained
1 can of corn, drained
1/2 cup of diced ham
1/4 cup of diced red bell pepper
1/4 cup of diced green bell pepper
1/4 cup of diced onion
1/2 cup of mayonnaise
Salt and pepper to taste

Instructions:

Boil the potatoes and carrots until they are tender. Drain and let them cool. In a bowl, mix the potatoes, carrots, peas, corn, ham, bell peppers, and onion together.
Add the mayonnaise and mix well. Season with salt and pepper to taste. Refrigerate for at least 30 minutes before serving.

ENSALADA DE PAPA Y ATÚN (POTATO AND TUNA SALAD)

Ingredients:

4 medium potatoes, peeled and cubed
2 cans of tuna, drained
1/2 cup of chopped onion
1/4 cup of chopped celery
1/4 cup of chopped red bell pepper
1/4 cup of chopped green bell pepper
1/2 cup of mayonnaise
1 tablespoon of mustard
Salt and pepper to taste

Instructions:

Boil the potatoes until they are tender. Drain and let them cool. In a bowl, mix the tuna, onion, celery, bell peppers, mayonnaise, and mustard together. Add the potatoes and mix well. Season with salt and pepper to taste. Refrigerate for at least 30 minutes before serving.

ENSALADA DE QUESO Y MENTA (CHEESE AND MINT SALAD)

Ingredients:

1 head of romaine lettuce, torn into bite-sized pieces
1 cup of diced fresh mozzarella cheese
1/4 cup of chopped fresh mint leaves
1/4 cup of chopped red onion
1/4 cup of olive oil
1/4 cup of red wine vinegar
1 tablespoon of honey
Salt and pepper to taste

Instructions:

In a large bowl, mix the lettuce, cheese, mint, and onion together. In a small bowl, whisk the olive oil, red wine vinegar, honey, salt, and pepper together. Pour the dressing over the salad and toss to coat. Refrigerate for at least 30 minutes before serving.

ENSALADA PRIMAVERAL DE PALMITO (SPRING PALM HEART SALAD)

Ingredients:

2 cans of palm hearts, drained and sliced
1 head of lettuce, washed and chopped
2 tomatoes, chopped
1 small red onion, chopped
1/2 cup of fresh parsley, chopped
1/4 cup of olive oil
2 tablespoons of white wine vinegar
1 tablespoon of honey
Salt and pepper to taste

Instructions:

In a large bowl, combine the sliced palm hearts, chopped lettuce, chopped tomatoes, chopped red onion, and chopped parsley. In a separate bowl, whisk together the olive oil, white wine vinegar, honey, salt, and pepper until well combined. Pour the dressing over the salad and toss well to coat all the ingredients. Serve immediately and enjoy your refreshing spring salad!

SOUPS

CAZUELITAS DE ATÚN (TUNA CASSEROLES)

Ingredients:

2 cans of tuna
2 tablespoons of mayonnaise
1 tablespoon of mustard
1 tablespoon of ketchup
1 onion, chopped
1 bell pepper, chopped
1 tomato, chopped
1/4 cup of grated cheese
Salt and pepper to taste

Instructions:

Preheat the oven to 350°F (180°C). In a bowl, mix the tuna, mayonnaise, mustard, ketchup, salt, and pepper until well combined. In another bowl, mix the chopped onion, bell pepper, and tomato. Grease 4 small baking dishes and distribute the tuna mixture evenly among them. Top the tuna mixture with the vegetable mixture and sprinkle the grated cheese on top. Bake for 20-25 minutes or until the cheese is melted and golden brown.

CREMA DE ZANAHORIA CON JENGIBRE (CARROT AND GINGER SOUP)

Ingredients:

4 cups of chopped carrots
1 onion, chopped
2 garlic cloves, minced
1 tablespoon of grated ginger
4 cups of chicken or vegetable broth
1/2 cup of heavy cream
Salt and pepper to taste

Instructions:

In a large pot, sauté the chopped onion and minced garlic until translucent. Add the chopped carrots and grated ginger to the pot and sauté for 5 minutes. Add the chicken or vegetable broth and bring to a boil. Reduce the heat and let it simmer for 15-20 minutes or until the carrots are soft. Using an immersion blender or transferring the mixture to a blender, puree the soup until smooth. Add the heavy cream and stir until well combined. Season with salt and pepper to taste.

CAZUELA DE MARISCOS (SEAFOOD CASSEROLE)

Ingredients:

1 pound of shrimp, peeled and deveined
1 pound of white fish, cut into bite-sized pieces
1/2 pound of squid, cut into rings
1 onion, chopped
1 red bell pepper, chopped
1 green bell pepper, chopped
4 garlic cloves, minced
1 can of diced tomatoes
1/2 cup of white wine
1/4 cup of chopped parsley
Salt and pepper to taste
Olive oil

Instructions:

In a large pot or Dutch oven, sauté the chopped onion and minced garlic in olive oil until translucent. Add the chopped bell peppers and sauté for 5 minutes. Add the diced tomatoes and white wine to the pot and bring to a simmer. Add the shrimp, white fish, and squid to the pot and cook for 5-7 minutes or until the seafood is cooked through. Season with salt and pepper to taste. Garnish with chopped parsley and serve hot.

CREMA DE ARVEJA
(PEA SOUP)

Ingredients:

2 cups dried split peas
8 cups water
1 onion, chopped
1 garlic clove, minced
1 tsp ground cumin
1 tsp salt
1/2 tsp black pepper
2 tbsp vegetable oil
1/4 cup cilantro, chopped

Instructions:

Rinse the split peas and soak them overnight in water. Drain the peas and add them to a pot with 8 cups of fresh water. Bring to a boil, then reduce the heat and simmer for 1-2 hours, or until the peas are tender. In a separate pan, sauté the onion, garlic, cumin, salt, and black pepper in the vegetable oil until the onion is soft and translucent. Add the sautéed mixture to the pot of peas and simmer for another 20-30 minutes. Use an immersion blender to blend the soup until it is smooth and creamy. Serve hot, garnished with cilantro.

SOPA FRÍA DE AGUACATE (COLD AVOCADO SOUP)

Ingredients:

2 ripe avocados, peeled and pitted
2 cups chicken broth
1 cup milk
1/2 cup sour cream
1/4 cup lime juice
1 garlic clove, minced
1/4 tsp ground cumin
Salt and pepper, to taste
Chopped cilantro and sliced avocado, for garnish

Instructions:

In a blender, puree the avocados, chicken broth, milk, sour cream, lime juice, garlic, cumin, salt, and pepper until smooth. Chill the soup in the refrigerator for at least 1 hour, or until cold. Serve in bowls, garnished with chopped cilantro and sliced avocado.

AJÍACO (CHICKEN AND POTATO SOUP)

Ingredients:

2 lbs chicken thighs
6 cups chicken broth
2 cups water
1 onion, chopped
4 garlic cloves, minced
4 Yukon gold potatoes, peeled and cubed
1 large ear of corn, cut into rounds
1/2 cup guascas (dried Andean herb)
1/2 cup heavy cream
1/4 cup capers, drained
Salt and pepper, to taste
Avocado, sliced, for garnish
Rice, cooked, for serving

Instructions:

In a large pot, add the chicken thighs, chicken broth, water, onion, and garlic. Bring to a boil, then reduce the heat and simmer for 30 minutes. Remove the chicken from the pot and shred the meat, discarding the bones and skin. Add the potatoes, corn, and guascas to the pot and simmer for 30 minutes, or until the potatoes are tender. Add the shredded chicken, heavy cream, and capers to the pot and stir to combine. Season with salt and pepper to taste. Serve hot, garnished with sliced avocado, and with cooked rice on the side.

CREMA DE CHOCLO (CREAM OF CORN SOUP)

Ingredients:

4 cups corn kernels
2 tablespoons butter
1/2 onion, chopped
2 garlic cloves, chopped
2 cups chicken broth
1 cup milk
Salt and pepper to taste
Chopped fresh cilantro (optional)

Instructions:

In a pot over medium heat, melt the butter and add the onion and garlic. Cook until the onion is translucent, about 5 minutes. Add the corn kernels and chicken broth to the pot. Bring to a boil and then reduce heat to low. Simmer for 15-20 minutes or until the corn is tender. Remove from heat and use an immersion blender or transfer to a blender to blend the soup until smooth. Return the blended soup to the pot over low heat. Add milk and stir until heated through. Season with salt and pepper to taste. Garnish with chopped cilantro if desired.

MONDONGO (TRIPE SOUP)

Ingredients:

2 pounds of beef tripe, cleaned and cut into small pieces
1/2 pound of pork belly or bacon, cut into small pieces
1/2 cup of chopped onion
1/4 cup of chopped green onion
2 garlic cloves, minced
1/4 cup of chopped cilantro
2 bay leaves
2 teaspoons of cumin
2 teaspoons of paprika
1/2 teaspoon of dried oregano
Salt and pepper to taste
6 cups of water or beef broth
1 cup of cooked white rice
1 lime, cut into wedges
Hot sauce (optional)

Instructions:

In a large pot, cook the tripe in boiling water for 15 minutes. Drain the tripe and rinse with cold water. In the same pot, add the pork belly or bacon and cook until crispy. Remove and set aside. Add the onion, green onion, garlic, and cilantro to the pot and sauté until the onion is translucent. Add the tripe and pork belly or bacon back to the pot along with the bay leaves, cumin, paprika, oregano, salt, and pepper. Stir to combine. Pour in the water or beef broth and bring to a boil. Reduce heat to low and let simmer for 2-3 hours or until the tripe is tender. Remove the bay leaves and adjust seasoning if needed. Serve the soup with cooked white rice, lime wedges, and hot sauce if desired.

CREMA DE CHAMPIÑONES (CREAM OF MUSHROOM SOUP)

Ingredients:

1 pound mushrooms, sliced
1 onion, chopped
2 cloves garlic, minced
4 cups chicken or vegetable broth
1 cup heavy cream
2 tablespoons butter
2 tablespoons flour
Salt and pepper to taste
Chopped fresh parsley for garnish

Instructions:

Melt the butter in a large pot over medium heat. Add the onions and garlic and cook until softened, about 5 minutes. Add the mushrooms and cook until they release their liquid and start to brown, about 10 minutes. Sprinkle the flour over the mushrooms and stir until well combined. Slowly add the broth while stirring constantly to prevent lumps from forming. Bring the soup to a boil, then reduce the heat and simmer for 20 minutes. Use an immersion blender or transfer the soup to a blender and blend until smooth. Return the soup to the pot and add the heavy cream. Heat until warmed through. Season with salt and pepper to taste.Garnish with chopped parsley before serving.

SOPA DE GUANDÚ (PIGEON PEA SOUP) RECIPE:

Ingredients:

2 cups dried pigeon peas (guandú), rinsed and drained
8 cups water
1 onion, chopped
2 cloves garlic, minced
1 green bell pepper, chopped
2 tomatoes, chopped
1 tablespoon olive oil
Salt and pepper to taste
Chopped fresh cilantro for garnish

Instructions:

In a large pot, combine the pigeon peas and water. Bring to a boil, then reduce the heat and simmer for 1 hour or until the peas are tender. In a separate pan, heat the olive oil over medium heat. Add the onion, garlic, and bell pepper and sauté until softened, about 5 minutes. Add the tomatoes and cook for another 5 minutes. Add the onion mixture to the pot with the pigeon peas and simmer for an additional 20 minutes. Use an immersion blender or transfer the soup to a blender and blend until smooth. Season with salt and pepper to taste. Garnish with chopped cilantro before serving.

SHRIMP SOUP

Ingredients:

1 lb raw shrimp, peeled and deveined
1 tbsp olive oil
1 onion, chopped
2 garlic cloves, minced
1 red bell pepper, chopped
1 green bell pepper, chopped
1 tomato, chopped
2 tbsp tomato paste
6 cups chicken or seafood broth
1 cup coconut milk
1 tsp cumin
1 tsp paprika
Salt and pepper to taste
Cilantro for garnish
Lime wedges for serving

Instructions:

Heat the olive oil in a large pot over medium heat. Add the onion and garlic and sauté for 2-3 minutes, until fragrant. Add the chopped bell peppers and tomato and cook for 5-6 minutes, until the vegetables are soft. Stir in the tomato paste, cumin, paprika, salt, and pepper and cook for 1-2 minutes. Pour in the chicken or seafood broth and bring to a boil. Reduce the heat to low and simmer for 10-15 minutes. Add the raw shrimp and cook for 3-4 minutes, until the shrimp are pink and cooked through. Stir in the coconut milk and cook for 1-2 minutes, until heated through. Garnish with cilantro and serve with lime wedges. Enjoy!

CREMA DE LANGOSTA, CAMARONES O LANGOSTINOS

Ingredients:

1 pound of lobster, shrimp or langoustine meat
1/4 cup of butter
1/4 cup of flour
2 cups of milk
2 cups of fish or seafood stock
1/4 cup of heavy cream
1/4 cup of sherry or white wine
Salt and pepper, to taste
Fresh parsley or chives, chopped (optional)

Instructions:

In a large pot, melt the butter over medium heat. Add the flour and stir constantly for 1-2 minutes until the mixture becomes a smooth paste. Gradually whisk in the milk and seafood stock, stirring constantly to prevent lumps from forming. Bring the mixture to a boil, then reduce the heat to low and let it simmer for 10-15 minutes, stirring occasionally. Add the lobster, shrimp or langoustine meat to the pot and let it simmer for an additional 10-15 minutes until the seafood is cooked through. Stir in the heavy cream and sherry or white wine, and season the soup with salt and pepper to taste. Serve the soup hot, garnished with fresh parsley or chives if desired.

MUTE SANTANDEREANO

Ingredients:

1 pound of beef tripe, cleaned and chopped into small pieces
1/2 pound of beef or pork belly, cut into small pieces
1/2 cup of chopped onion
1/4 cup of chopped scallions
2 garlic cloves, minced
2 cups of diced potatoes
2 cups of diced yucca or cassava root
1/4 cup of chopped cilantro
1/4 cup of chopped parsley
1 teaspoon of ground cumin
1 teaspoon of ground achiote or annatto
8 cups of beef broth or water
Salt and pepper, to taste
Fried pork rinds (chicharrón) and avocado, for serving (optional)

Instructions:

In a large pot, bring the beef broth or water to a boil. Add the beef tripe, beef or pork belly, onion, scallions and garlic, and let it simmer for 1-2 hours until the meat is tender. Add the diced potatoes and yucca or cassava root to the pot, along with the chopped cilantro, parsley, cumin and achiote. Simmer for an additional 30-40 minutes until the vegetables are soft and the soup has thickened. Season the soup with salt and pepper to taste, and serve hot with fried pork rinds and avocado slices on top, if desired.

SOPA DE MANZANA
(APPLE SOUP)

Ingredients:

3 apples, peeled and diced
2 tablespoons unsalted butter
1 onion, diced
2 cups chicken or vegetable broth
1/2 cup heavy cream
Salt and pepper to taste
Chives, chopped (for garnish)

Instructions:

Melt the butter in a large pot over medium heat. Add the onion and cook until translucent, about 5 minutes. Add the apples and cook for another 5 minutes, stirring occasionally. Add the broth and bring to a simmer. Cook until the apples are tender, about 10-15 minutes. Remove from heat and let cool for a few minutes. Blend the soup in a blender or food processor until smooth. Return the soup to the pot and stir in the heavy cream. Reheat the soup over low heat, stirring occasionally. Season with salt and pepper to taste. Serve hot, garnished with chopped chives.

SOPA DE TOMATE AL LAUREL (TOMATO SOUP WITH BAY LEAF)

Ingredients:

2 tablespoons olive oil
1 onion, chopped
2 cloves garlic, minced
6 tomatoes, chopped
2 cups chicken or vegetable broth
1 bay leaf
1/4 cup heavy cream
Salt and pepper to taste
Fresh basil, chopped (for garnish)

Instructions:

Heat the olive oil in a large pot over medium heat. Add the onion and garlic and cook until softened, about 5 minutes. Add the chopped tomatoes and cook for another 5 minutes. Add the broth and bay leaf and bring to a simmer. Cook until the tomatoes are tender, about 15-20 minutes. Remove from heat and let cool for a few minutes. Remove the bay leaf and blend the soup in a blender or food processor until smooth. Return the soup to the pot and stir in the heavy cream. Reheat the soup over low heat, stirring occasionally. Season with salt and pepper to taste. Serve hot, garnished with chopped fresh basil.

CALDO DE QUESO Y CEBOLLAS (CHEESE AND ONION SOUP)

Ingredients:

2 tablespoons unsalted butter
2 onions, thinly sliced
4 cups chicken or vegetable broth
1 cup heavy cream
1 cup grated cheese (such as cheddar or Gouda)
Salt and pepper to taste
Chives, chopped (for garnish)

Instructions:

Melt the butter in a large pot over medium heat. Add the onions and cook until softened, about 5 minutes. Add the broth and bring to a simmer. Cook until the onions are tender, about 15-20 minutes. Remove from heat and let cool for a few minutes. Blend the soup in a blender or food processor until smooth. Return the soup to the pot and stir in the heavy cream and grated cheese.Reheat the soup over low heat, stirring occasionally, until the cheese is melted and the soup is heated through. Season with salt and pepper to taste.

Serve hot, garnished with chopped chives.

CREMA CAMPESTRE

Ingredients:

1 tablespoon vegetable oil
1 large onion, chopped
3 garlic cloves, minced
2 large potatoes, peeled and diced
2 cups corn kernels
4 cups chicken or vegetable broth
1/2 cup heavy cream
Salt and pepper, to taste
1/4 cup chopped fresh parsley

Instructions:

Heat the vegetable oil in a large pot over medium heat. Add the onion and garlic and sauté until softened, about 5 minutes. Add the potatoes and corn to the pot, and stir to combine. Pour in the chicken or vegetable broth and bring the mixture to a boil. Reduce the heat and simmer for 20-25 minutes, or until the vegetables are tender. Use an immersion blender or transfer the soup to a blender and puree until smooth. Stir in the heavy cream and season with salt and pepper to taste. Ladle the soup into bowls and garnish with fresh parsley.

Enjoy your delicious Crema Campestre!

CREMA DE CALABAZA Y QUINUA CON QUESO

Ingredients:

1/2 cup quinoa
2 cups water
2 tablespoons olive oil
1 onion, chopped
2 garlic cloves, minced
1 teaspoon cumin
4 cups chopped pumpkin or squash
4 cups chicken or vegetable broth
Salt and pepper, to taste
1/2 cup grated cheese (queso fresco, feta, or parmesan)

Instructions:

Rinse the quinoa in a fine mesh strainer and place it in a saucepan with 2 cups of water. Bring to a boil, then reduce the heat and let simmer for 15-20 minutes, or until the quinoa is cooked and the water has been absorbed. In a large pot, heat the olive oil over medium heat. Add the onion and sauté for 3-4 minutes, until it starts to soften. Add the garlic and cumin and cook for another minute. Add the chopped pumpkin or squash to the pot and sauté for 5-7 minutes, until it starts to brown and soften. Add the chicken or vegetable broth to the pot and bring to a boil. Reduce the heat and let simmer for 20-30 minutes, until the pumpkin or squash is tender. Use an immersion blender or transfer the soup to a blender and puree until smooth. Add the cooked quinoa to the soup and stir to combine. Season with salt and pepper, to taste. Serve hot, topped with grated cheese.

CALDO DE GUACUCO

Ingredients:

2 lbs of guacuco clams
4 cups of water
1 onion, chopped
1 tomato, chopped
1 bell pepper, chopped
2 garlic cloves, minced
1 tsp of ground cumin
1 tsp of ground annatto (achiote)
1 tsp of dried oregano
1 tsp of salt
1/4 tsp of black pepper
1/4 cup of chopped cilantro
2 limes, cut into wedges

Instructions:

Clean the guacuco clams by rinsing them under cold running water and removing any dirt or debris. Soak them in cold water for about 30 minutes to release any sand or grit. In a large pot, add the water, onion, tomato, bell pepper, garlic, cumin, annatto, oregano, salt, and black pepper. Bring to a boil and then reduce heat to medium. Add the guacuco clams to the pot and stir well. Cover the pot and let the clams cook for about 15-20 minutes, until they open up. Remove any clams that have not opened and discard them. Serve the soup hot, garnished with cilantro and lime wedges. Enjoy your delicious Caldo de Guacuco!

SOPA DE ALMEJAS (CLAM SOUP)

Ingredients:

2 lbs of clams in shells, scrubbed
2 tablespoons of butter
1 large onion, finely chopped
3 cloves of garlic, minced
2 large potatoes, peeled and diced
2 cups of chicken or fish broth
1 cup of heavy cream
Salt and pepper to taste
Chopped fresh parsley for garnish

Instructions:

In a large pot, melt the butter over medium heat. Add the onion and garlic and sauté until the onion is translucent, about 5 minutes. Add the diced potatoes and broth, and bring to a boil. Reduce heat and simmer until the potatoes are tender, about 15-20 minutes. Add the clams and continue to simmer until the clams have opened, about 5-10 minutes. Remove any clams that haven't opened. Stir in the heavy cream and season with salt and pepper to taste. Garnish with fresh chopped parsley and serve hot.

MOTE DE QUESO

Ingredients:

2 cups of mote (hominy), cooked
2 cups of grated cheese (queso fresco, queso blanco, or a combination)
1 tablespoon of butter
1 small onion, finely chopped
2 garlic cloves, minced
2 cups of milk
Salt and pepper to taste
Chopped fresh cilantro for garnish

Instructions:

In a large saucepan, melt the butter over medium heat. Add the onion and garlic and sauté until the onion is translucent, about 5 minutes. Add the cooked mote and grated cheese, stirring until the cheese is melted and well combined. Pour in the milk and stir to combine. Simmer over low heat, stirring occasionally, until the mote is tender and the mixture has thickened, about 15-20 minutes. Season with salt and pepper to taste. Garnish with fresh chopped cilantro and serve hot.

SANCOCHO DE CERDO SALADO

Ingredients:

2 lbs of salt pork or pork belly
1 lb of yuca, peeled and cut into chunks
1 lb of potatoes, peeled and cut into chunks
2 ears of corn, cut into chunks
2 green plantains, peeled and cut into chunks
1 onion, finely chopped
3 cloves of garlic, minced
2 tablespoons of vegetable oil
8 cups of water
Salt and pepper to taste
Chopped fresh cilantro for garnish

Instructions:

In a large pot, heat the vegetable oil over medium-high heat. Add the pork and brown on all sides. Add the onion and garlic and sauté until the onion is translucent, about 5 minutes. Add the water and bring to a boil. Reduce heat to medium-low and simmer for 30 minutes. Add the yuca and simmer for 10 minutes. Add the potatoes and corn and simmer for another 10 minutes. Finally, add the plantains and simmer until all the vegetables are tender, about 10-15 minutes more. Season with salt and pepper to taste. Garnish with fresh chopped cilantro and serve hot.

CALDO DE HUEVO (EGG SOUP)

Ingredients:

4 cups of chicken broth
4 eggs
1/4 cup of chopped cilantro
1/2 cup of diced onion
2 garlic cloves, minced
Salt and pepper to taste

Instructions:

In a medium pot, bring the chicken broth to a boil over medium-high heat. In a separate bowl, beat the eggs until smooth. Add the cilantro, onion, garlic, salt, and pepper to the eggs and mix well. Slowly pour the egg mixture into the boiling broth while stirring constantly. Reduce heat to low and simmer for 5-10 minutes until the eggs are fully cooked. Serve hot with bread or crackers.

SANCOCHO DE PATO (DUCK SANCOCHO)

Ingredients:

1 whole duck, cut into pieces
8 cups of water
1 cup of chopped onion
1 cup of chopped tomato
1 cup of chopped bell pepper
1 cup of chopped cilantro
1/2 cup of chopped scallions
4 garlic cloves, minced
1/4 cup of grated cassava or yucca
1/4 cup of chopped fresh oregano
Salt and pepper to taste
2 green plantains, peeled and cut into chunks
2 ripe plantains, peeled and cut into chunks
2 yuca roots, peeled and cut into chunks
1 corn on the cob, cut into pieces
1 avocado, peeled and sliced (for garnish)
1 lime, cut into wedges (for garnish)

Instructions:

In a large pot, bring the duck pieces and water to a boil over medium-high heat. Skim off any foam that rises to the surface and discard. Add the onion, tomato, bell pepper, cilantro, scallions, garlic, cassava, oregano, salt, and pepper to the pot and stir well. Reduce heat to medium-low and let simmer for 1 hour, stirring occasionally. Add the green and ripe plantains, yuca, and corn to the pot and continue simmering for another 30-45 minutes until the vegetables are tender. Serve hot in bowls with avocado slices and lime wedges on the side. Enjoy!

ABORRAJADOS DE PESCADO (FRIED PLANTAIN STUFFED WITH FISH)

Ingredients:

4 ripe plantains
1 lb white fish fillet, cut into small pieces
1 onion, finely chopped
2 garlic cloves, minced
1 red bell pepper, finely chopped
1 tsp cumin
1 tsp oregano
Salt and pepper, to taste
2 cups vegetable oil, for frying

Instructions:

Peel the plantains and cut them in half. Cut each half into thin slices lengthwise. In a pan, sauté the onion, garlic, and red bell pepper until they are soft. Add the fish, cumin, oregano, salt, and pepper. Cook until the fish is cooked through. Take a slice of plantain and place a spoonful of the fish mixture on top. Place another slice on top and press down to seal. Heat the oil in a pan over medium heat. Fry the aborrajados until golden brown on both sides.
Remove from the oil and place on paper towels to remove excess oil. Serve hot.

ACORDA DE LANGOSTINOS (SHRIMP SOUP WITH BREAD)

Ingredients:

1 lb shrimp, peeled and deveined
4 garlic cloves, minced
1 onion, finely chopped
1 red bell pepper, finely chopped
2 tomatoes, chopped
1/2 cup fresh cilantro, chopped
1/2 cup olive oil
4 cups fish or vegetable stock
1 baguette, sliced
Salt and pepper, to taste

Instructions:

In a pan, sauté the garlic, onion, and red bell pepper until they are soft. Add the tomatoes and cook for a few minutes. Add the shrimp and cook until they turn pink.
Add the cilantro, salt, and pepper. In another pot, bring the stock to a boil. Add the sautéed shrimp mixture to the boiling stock and let it simmer for about 10 minutes. In a bowl, place a few slices of baguette and pour the soup on top. Drizzle with olive oil and serve hot.

MAIN DISHES

SALPICÓN DE ATÚN
(TUNA SALAD)

Ingredients:

2 cans of tuna in water, drained
1 red onion, finely chopped
1 red bell pepper, finely chopped
1 green bell pepper, finely chopped
1 cup cherry tomatoes, halved
1/2 cup fresh cilantro, chopped
1/4 cup lime juice
2 tbsp olive oil
Salt and pepper, to taste

Instructions:

In a bowl, mix the tuna, red onion, red and green bell peppers, cherry tomatoes, and cilantro. In a separate bowl, whisk together the lime juice, olive oil, salt, and pepper.
Pour the dressing over the tuna mixture and toss to combine. Serve chilled.

ARROZ CON CHAMPIÑONES (MUSHROOM RICE)

Ingredients:

2 cups long-grain white rice
4 cups chicken or vegetable broth
1 tablespoon olive oil
2 tablespoons unsalted butter
1 small onion, finely chopped
1 clove garlic, minced
1 pound fresh mushrooms, sliced
Salt and pepper, to taste
2 tablespoons chopped fresh parsley (optional)

Instructions:

Rinse the rice under cold water until the water runs clear. Drain and set aside. In a large pot or Dutch oven, heat the olive oil and butter over medium heat. Add the onion and garlic and sauté until the onion is soft and translucent, about 5 minutes. Add the mushrooms and sauté until they release their liquid and start to brown, about 10 minutes. Add the rice and stir to coat with the mushroom mixture. Pour in the broth and stir to combine. Season with salt and pepper. Bring to a boil, then reduce the heat to low, cover, and simmer until the rice is tender and the liquid is absorbed, about 18-20 minutes. Remove from heat and let the rice sit covered for 5 minutes. Fluff the rice with a fork, garnish with parsley (if desired), and serve.

CHAMPIÑONES AL AJO (GARLIC MUSHROOMS)

Ingredients:

1 pound fresh mushrooms, sliced
2 cloves garlic, minced
2 tablespoons olive oil
Salt and pepper, to taste
1 tablespoon chopped fresh parsley (optional)

Instructions:

In a large skillet, heat the olive oil over medium-high heat. Add the garlic and sauté for 30 seconds, until fragrant. Add the mushrooms and sauté until they release their liquid and start to brown, about 10-12 minutes. Season with salt and pepper to taste. Garnish with chopped parsley (if desired) and serve.

CHICHARRONES DE TOCINO (BACON CRACKLINGS)

Ingredients:

1 pound bacon
Water

Instructions:

Cut the bacon into small pieces and place them in a large pot or Dutch oven. Cover the bacon with water and bring to a boil over high heat. Reduce the heat to medium-low and let the bacon simmer for 45 minutes to 1 hour, until it is very tender. Remove the bacon from the pot and place it on a cutting board. Chop the bacon into small pieces and spread them out on a baking sheet. Bake in a 375°F oven for 10-15 minutes, until the bacon is crispy and golden brown. Drain on paper towels and serve.

CHAMPIÑONES AL AJO

Ingredients:

1 pound fresh mushrooms, sliced
4 tablespoons butter
4 cloves garlic, minced
1/4 cup chopped fresh parsley
Salt and black pepper to taste

Instructions:

In a large skillet, melt the butter over medium-high heat. Add the garlic and cook for about 1 minute or until fragrant. Add the sliced mushrooms and cook for 5-7 minutes, stirring occasionally, until they are tender and browned. Season with salt and pepper, to taste. Remove from heat and stir in the chopped parsley. Serve hot as a side dish.

CHICHARRONES DE TOCINO

Ingredients:

1 pound thick-cut bacon
2 tablespoons brown sugar
1 tablespoon smoked paprika
1/2 teaspoon garlic powder
1/4 teaspoon cayenne pepper
Salt and black pepper to taste

Instructions:

Preheat the oven to 375°F. In a small bowl, mix together the brown sugar, smoked paprika, garlic powder, cayenne pepper, salt, and black pepper. Place the bacon slices on a baking sheet lined with parchment paper. Sprinkle the spice mixture over the bacon slices, making sure to coat them evenly. Bake in the preheated oven for 20-25 minutes, or until the bacon is crispy and browned. Remove from the oven and let cool for a few minutes before serving.

COLOMBINITAS DE POLLO

Ingredients:

1 pound ground chicken
1/2 cup cooked white rice
1/2 cup cooked yellow cornmeal
1/2 cup grated Parmesan cheese
1/4 cup finely chopped onion
2 garlic cloves, minced
1 tablespoon chopped fresh cilantro
1 teaspoon ground cumin
Salt and black pepper to taste
Vegetable oil, for frying

Instructions:

In a large bowl, mix together the ground chicken, cooked rice, cooked cornmeal, Parmesan cheese, onion, garlic, cilantro, cumin, salt, and black pepper. Use your hands to form the mixture into small balls about the size of a golf ball. Heat the vegetable oil in a large skillet over medium-high heat. Add the chicken balls to the skillet and cook for 5-7 minutes, turning occasionally, until they are browned on all sides and cooked through. Remove from the skillet and place on a paper towel-lined plate to drain excess oil. Serve hot as a snack or appetizer.

GARBANZOS A LA MALLORQUINA (MALLORCAN-STYLE CHICKPEAS)

Ingredients:

2 cups cooked chickpeas (canned or cooked from dry)
2 cups spinach leaves, chopped
1 large onion, chopped
3 cloves garlic, minced
1 red bell pepper, chopped
1 green bell pepper, chopped
2 tomatoes, chopped
1/2 tsp smoked paprika
Salt and pepper to taste
Olive oil for cooking

Instructions:

In a large skillet, heat the olive oil over medium heat. Add the onion and garlic and sauté until softened. Add the bell peppers and cook until slightly softened. Add the chopped tomatoes and smoked paprika, and cook for 5-7 minutes, until the tomatoes are soft and pulpy. Add the cooked chickpeas and spinach, and stir until the spinach has wilted. Season with salt and pepper to taste, and serve.

ROLLITOS DE LECHUGA CON POLLO (CHICKEN LETTUCE WRAPS)

Ingredients:

1 lb ground chicken
2 tbsp vegetable oil
1 large onion, chopped
1 red bell pepper, chopped
3 cloves garlic, minced
1 tbsp grated ginger
2 tbsp soy sauce
2 tbsp hoisin sauce
2 tbsp oyster sauce
1 head of lettuce, leaves separated and washed

Instructions:

Heat the oil in a large skillet over medium-high heat. Add the onion and bell pepper, and sauté until slightly softened. Add the garlic and ginger, and sauté for another minute. Add the ground chicken, and cook until browned and cooked through. Add the soy sauce, hoisin sauce, and oyster sauce, and stir until everything is well combined and heated through. Remove from heat, and spoon the chicken mixture onto individual lettuce leaves. Roll up the lettuce leaves to make the wraps, and serve.

CAMARONES EN APURO (HURRY-UP SHRIMP)

Ingredients:

1 lb medium shrimp, peeled and deveined
2 tbsp olive oil
3 cloves garlic, minced
1/4 tsp red pepper flakes
Salt and pepper to taste
Lemon wedges for serving

Instructions:

Heat the olive oil in a large skillet over medium heat. Add the garlic and red pepper flakes, and sauté for 1-2 minutes until fragrant. Add the shrimp, and cook for 3-4 minutes on each side until pink and cooked through. Season with salt and pepper to taste. Serve hot with lemon wedges.

PATACONES CON TOMATE

Ingredients:

4 green plantains
2 medium tomatoes, diced
1/2 small red onion, finely chopped
1/4 cup fresh cilantro leaves, chopped
2 tablespoons olive oil
Salt and pepper to taste

Instructions:

Peel the plantains and cut them into 1 inch thick slices.
Heat the olive oil in a large frying pan over medium-high heat. Fry the plantain slices until they are golden brown, about 2-3 minutes per side. Remove the plantains from the pan and place them on a paper towel to drain the excess oil. In a small bowl, mix the diced tomatoes, chopped red onion, cilantro, salt, and pepper. Serve the patacones with the tomato mixture on top.

PATACONAS DESMECHADAS

Ingredients:

4 green plantains
2 cups shredded cooked beef or chicken
1/2 small red onion, finely chopped
1/4 cup fresh cilantro leaves, chopped
2 tablespoons olive oil
Salt and pepper to taste

Instructions:

Peel the plantains and cut them into 1 inch thick slices. Heat the olive oil in a large frying pan over medium-high heat. Fry the plantain slices until they are golden brown, about 2-3 minutes per side. Remove the plantains from the pan and place them on a paper towel to drain the excess oil. Using a fork, smash each plantain slice until it is flattened and about 1/4 inch thick. In a separate bowl, mix the shredded meat, chopped red onion, cilantro, salt, and pepper. Place a spoonful of the meat mixture on top of each flattened plantain slice. Fold the plantain slice in half to form a patacona. Serve the pataconas warm.

CEVICHE DE QUESOS

Ingredients:

1/2 pound feta cheese, cubed
1/2 pound mozzarella cheese, cubed
1/2 pound panela cheese, cubed
1 small red onion, finely chopped
1/4 cup fresh cilantro leaves, chopped
2 tablespoons olive oil
Juice of 1 lime
Salt and pepper to taste

Instructions:

In a large bowl, mix the cubed cheeses, chopped red onion, and chopped cilantro. Drizzle the olive oil and lime juice over the cheese mixture and mix well. Season with salt and pepper to taste. Cover the bowl and refrigerate for at least 1 hour to allow the flavors to meld together.Serve the ceviche de quesos cold, with crackers or bread on the side.

HUEVOS CON BECHAMEL

Ingredients:

4 large eggs
1 tablespoon butter
1 tablespoon all-purpose flour
1 cup milk
Salt and pepper to taste
Grated nutmeg (optional)
1/4 cup grated Parmesan cheese

Instructions:

In a saucepan, melt the butter over medium heat. Add the flour and stir until well combined. Gradually whisk in the milk, stirring constantly until the mixture thickens.
Season with salt, pepper, and nutmeg if using. Preheat the oven to 375°F. Grease four small oven-safe ramekins with butter. Crack an egg into each ramekin and pour the bechamel sauce on top. Sprinkle grated Parmesan cheese on top of the sauce. Bake in the preheated oven for 15-20 minutes or until the egg whites are set and the yolks are still runny. Serve immediately.

POLLO AL JENGIBRE

Ingredients:

4 boneless, skinless chicken breasts
Salt and pepper to taste
1/4 cup olive oil
2 tablespoons fresh ginger, peeled and grated
2 garlic cloves, minced
1/4 cup soy sauce
2 tablespoons honey
1 tablespoon cornstarch
1/4 cup water
2 green onions, thinly sliced

Instructions:

Preheat the oven to 375°F. Season the chicken breasts with salt and pepper. In a large oven-safe skillet, heat the olive oil over medium-high heat. Add the chicken breasts and cook until browned on both sides, about 3-4 minutes per side. Remove the chicken from the skillet and set aside. Add the ginger and garlic to the skillet and cook until fragrant, about 1 minute. Add the soy sauce and honey to the skillet and stir to combine. Return the chicken to the skillet and spoon the sauce over the chicken. Transfer the skillet to the preheated oven and bake for 20-25 minutes or until the chicken is cooked through. In a small bowl, whisk together the cornstarch and water. Remove the skillet from the oven and place it on the stovetop. Stir in the cornstarch mixture and cook over medium heat until the sauce thickens, about 2-3 minutes. Garnish with sliced green onions and serve.

FRICASE DE POLLO Y TOCINO (CHICKEN AND BACON FRICASSEE) FROM COLOMBIA:

Ingredients:

1 lb chicken thighs, bone-in and skin-on
4 slices bacon, chopped
1 onion, chopped
2 garlic cloves, minced
1/2 red bell pepper, sliced
1/2 green bell pepper, sliced
1 tbsp tomato paste
1/2 cup chicken broth
1/2 cup white wine
1 bay leaf
1 tsp oregano
1/2 tsp cumin
1/2 tsp paprika
Salt and pepper to taste
1 tbsp vegetable oil
2 tbsp chopped fresh parsley, for garnish

Instructions:

Season the chicken thighs with salt and pepper. Heat the vegetable oil in a large pot over medium-high heat. Add the chicken and brown on both sides, about 5-7 minutes per side. Remove the chicken from the pot and set aside.
In the same pot, add the bacon and sauté until crispy. Remove the bacon with a slotted spoon and set aside. Add the onion and garlic to the pot and sauté until softened, about 2-3 minutes. Add the red and green bell peppers and sauté for an additional

2-3 minutes. Stir in the tomato paste, chicken broth, white wine, bay leaf, oregano, cumin, and paprika. Bring to a simmer and cook for 5 minutes. Return the chicken and bacon to the pot and stir to combine. Cover and simmer for 30-40 minutes, or until the chicken is cooked through and tender. Remove the bay leaf and discard. Serve hot, garnished with chopped parsley.

CREPES DE POLLO, CHAMPIÑÓN Y MANÍ (CHICKEN, MUSHROOM, AND PEANUT CREPES):

Ingredients:

1 cup of all-purpose flour
2 eggs
1 1/4 cups of milk
1/4 teaspoon of salt
1/4 teaspoon of black pepper
2 tablespoons of butter
1 tablespoon of olive oil
1/2 cup of chopped onion
2 cloves of garlic, minced
1/2 pound of boneless, skinless chicken breast, cut into small pieces
1/2 pound of mushrooms, sliced
1/2 cup of chopped roasted peanuts
Salt and black pepper to taste
1/4 cup of chopped fresh parsley
1/4 cup of grated Parmesan cheese

Instructions:

In a bowl, whisk together the flour, eggs, milk, salt, and pepper until you get a smooth batter. Heat a small non-stick skillet over medium-high heat and melt 1/2 tablespoon of butter. Add 1/4 cup of the batter and swirl the skillet to coat the bottom evenly. Cook for 1-2 minutes until the crepe is set and lightly golden. Flip the crepe and cook for another 30 seconds. Transfer the crepe to a plate and repeat with the remaining batter until you have 8 crepes. In a large skillet, heat the olive oil over medium heat. Add the onion and garlic and cook for 2-3 minutes until soft and fragrant. Add the chicken and cook for 5-6 minutes until golden and cooked through. Add the mushrooms and cook for another 5-6 minutes until soft and lightly browned. Add the chopped peanuts and season with salt and black pepper to taste. Stir in the parsley and Parmesan cheese. Divide the chicken and mushroom mixture evenly among the crepes and roll them up. Serve hot. Enjoy!

SOBREBARRIGA EN SALSA

Ingredients:

1.5-2 lbs beef flank or brisket
1 onion, chopped
4 garlic cloves, minced
1 red bell pepper, chopped
2 tomatoes, chopped
2 tbsp tomato paste
2 cups beef broth
1 tbsp cumin
1 tbsp paprika
Salt and pepper, to taste
Vegetable oil

Instructions:

Preheat oven to 350°F. Season the beef with salt and pepper. In a large oven-safe pot or Dutch oven, heat the oil over medium-high heat. Add the beef and sear until browned on all sides, about 5 minutes per side. Remove the beef from the pot and set aside. Add the onion, garlic, and red bell pepper to the pot and sauté until softened, about 5 minutes. Add the tomatoes, tomato paste, beef broth, cumin, paprika, and additional salt and pepper to the pot. Stir well to combine. Return the beef to the pot, making sure it is fully submerged in the liquid. Cover the pot with a lid and transfer to the oven. Bake for 2-3 hours, or until the beef is tender and can be easily shredded with a fork. Remove the pot from the oven and use two forks to shred the beef in the pot. Serve hot with rice, beans, and/or a salad. Enjoy!

PICADILLO

Ingredients:

1 lb ground beef
1 onion, chopped
2 cloves garlic, minced
1 red bell pepper, chopped
1 green bell pepper, chopped
1 tomato, chopped
1 tbsp tomato paste
1 tsp ground cumin
1 tsp dried oregano
1/4 cup raisins
1/4 cup pimento-stuffed green olives
Salt and pepper to taste
2 tbsp olive oil

Instructions:

Heat the olive oil in a large skillet over medium heat. Add the onion, garlic, red and green bell peppers, and tomato. Cook for 5 minutes or until the vegetables are soft. Add the ground beef and cook, stirring frequently, until the beef is browned and crumbled. Add the tomato paste, cumin, oregano, raisins, and olives. Stir to combine. Season with salt and pepper to taste. Reduce heat to low and simmer for 10-15 minutes. Serve hot with rice or as a filling for empanadas.

LENTEJAS A LA CRIOLLA

Ingredients:

2 cups dried lentils
6 cups water
2 tbsp olive oil
1 onion, chopped
2 cloves garlic, minced
1 red bell pepper, chopped
1 green bell pepper, chopped
1 tomato, chopped
2 tbsp tomato paste
1 tsp ground cumin
1 tsp paprika
2 bay leaves
Salt and pepper to taste
1/4 cup chopped fresh cilantro

Instructions:

Rinse the lentils in a fine mesh strainer and discard any stones or debris. In a large pot, bring the water to a boil. Add the lentils and reduce heat to low. Simmer for 20-25 minutes or until the lentils are tender. In a separate pan, heat the olive oil over medium heat. Add the onion, garlic, red and green bell peppers, and tomato. Cook for 5 minutes or until the vegetables are soft. Add the tomato paste, cumin, paprika, bay leaves, salt, and pepper. Stir to combine. Add the cooked lentils to the pan with the vegetables and stir to combine. Simmer for 10-15 minutes to allow the flavors to meld. Remove the bay leaves and discard. Serve hot, garnished with chopped cilantro.

PIPITORIA DE CHIVO

Ingredients:

2 pounds of goat meat
1 onion, diced
2 cloves of garlic, minced
1 red bell pepper, diced
1 green bell pepper, diced
2 tomatoes, diced
2 tablespoons of vegetable oil
1 teaspoon of ground cumin
1 teaspoon of ground coriander
1 teaspoon of ground achiote
1/2 teaspoon of ground cloves
Salt and pepper to taste
2 cups of water
2 tablespoons of cornstarch
1/2 cup of capers
1/2 cup of green olives, sliced
1/4 cup of raisins
1/4 cup of almonds, sliced

Instructions:

Cut the goat meat into small cubes and season with salt and pepper. Heat the vegetable oil in a large pot over medium heat. Add the goat meat and brown on all sides. Add the onion, garlic, red and green bell peppers, and tomatoes to the pot. Cook until the vegetables are softened. Add the cumin, coriander, achiote, and cloves to the pot and stir to combine. Pour in the water and bring to a boil. Reduce heat and simmer for about an hour, or until the goat meat is tender. In a small bowl, whisk together the cornstarch with a few tablespoons of water until smooth. Add the cornstarch mixture to the pot and stir well. Cook for another few minutes, or until the sauce has thickened. Add the capers, olives, raisins, and almonds to the pot and stir to combine. Cook for another 10-15 minutes, or until everything is heated through and the flavors have melded together. Serve hot with rice or mashed potatoes.

BANDEJA PAISA

Ingredients:

1 pound of ground beef
1 pound of chorizo sausage
1 pound of pork belly or bacon
1 pound of cooked red beans
4 plantains, peeled and sliced lengthwise
4 eggs, fried or scrambled
1 avocado, sliced
2 cups of cooked white rice
1 onion, diced
2 tomatoes, diced
1/2 cup of chopped cilantro
2 tablespoons of vegetable oil
Salt and pepper to taste

Instructions:

In a large skillet, cook the ground beef over medium heat until browned. Remove from skillet and set aside. In the same skillet, cook the chorizo and pork belly or bacon until browned and crispy. Remove from skillet and set aside. In the same skillet, cook the sliced plantains until golden brown on both sides. Remove from skillet and set aside. In a separate skillet, fry or scramble the eggs. In a large serving dish, arrange the cooked beef, chorizo, and pork belly or bacon. Add the cooked red beans, cooked white rice, and fried or scrambled eggs. Top with the sliced avocado, diced onion, diced tomatoes, and chopped cilantro. Serve hot with the fried plantains on the side.

LOMITO DE CERDO CON SALSA DE PAPAYA (PORK TENDERLOIN WITH PAPAYA SAUCE)

Ingredients:

2 pork tenderloins (about 1 pound each)
1 tablespoon ground cumin
1 tablespoon chili powder
1 tablespoon paprika
1 tablespoon dried oregano
1 teaspoon salt
1/2 teaspoon black pepper
2 tablespoons olive oil
2 cups diced ripe papaya
1/2 cup diced red onion
1/4 cup chopped fresh cilantro
2 tablespoons fresh lime juice
Salt and pepper to taste

Instructions:

Preheat oven to 375°F (190°C). In a small bowl, mix together cumin, chili powder, paprika, oregano, salt, and black pepper. Rub the spice mixture all over the pork tenderloins. Heat the olive oil in a large ovenproof skillet over medium-high heat. Add the pork tenderloins and sear for 2-3 minutes on each side until browned. Transfer the skillet to the oven and roast the pork for 15-20 minutes, until it reaches an internal temperature of 145°F (63°C). Meanwhile, in a medium bowl, mix together papaya, red onion, cilantro, and lime juice. Season with salt and pepper to taste. Let the pork rest for 5 minutes before slicing it into 1/2-inch-thick slices. Serve with the papaya salsa on the side.

MACARRONES CON VERDURAS (MACARONI WITH VEGETABLES):

Ingredients:

500g macaroni
1 red bell pepper, diced
1 green bell pepper, diced
1 onion, diced
2 zucchinis, diced
1 can of crushed tomatoes
3 cloves of garlic, minced
1/4 cup of olive oil
Salt and pepper to taste

Instructions:

Cook macaroni according to package instructions. Drain and set aside. In a large skillet, heat olive oil over medium heat. Add garlic and onion and cook until onion is translucent. Add bell peppers and zucchinis and cook until they are tender. Add crushed tomatoes and simmer for 5-10 minutes. Season with salt and pepper to taste. Add the cooked macaroni to the skillet and stir well. Serve hot.

PATACONES ESPECIALES (SPECIAL FRIED PLANTAINS)

Ingredients:

2 green plantains
1/2 cup vegetable oil
Salt to taste

Instructions:

Peel the plantains and cut them into 1-inch slices. Heat the vegetable oil in a large skillet over medium-high heat.
Fry the plantain slices until they are golden brown, about 3-4 minutes per side. Remove the plantains from the skillet and place them on a paper towel to remove excess oil.
Using a tostonera (plantain press), flatten the plantains.
Fry the flattened plantains again for 2-3 minutes on each side, until they are crispy and golden brown. Remove from the skillet and sprinkle with salt to taste. Serve hot.

SALMÓN AL WHISKY (WHISKEY SALMON)

Ingredients:

4 salmon fillets
Salt and pepper to taste
1/4 cup whiskey
1/4 cup soy sauce
2 tablespoons honey
2 tablespoons olive oil
2 garlic cloves, minced
2 tablespoons chopped fresh parsley

Instructions:

Preheat oven to 400°F. Season salmon fillets with salt and pepper on both sides. In a small bowl, whisk together whiskey, soy sauce, honey, olive oil, garlic, and parsley. Place salmon fillets in a baking dish and pour the whiskey mixture over them. Bake in the preheated oven for 12-15 minutes, until the salmon is cooked through. Serve hot.

PATACONES ESPECIALES (SPECIAL FRIED PLANTAINS)

Ingredients:

2 green plantains
1/2 cup vegetable oil
Salt to taste

Instructions:

Peel the plantains and cut them into 1-inch slices. Heat the vegetable oil in a large skillet over medium-high heat.
Fry the plantain slices until they are golden brown, about 3-4 minutes per side. Remove the plantains from the skillet and place them on a paper towel to remove excess oil.
Using a tostonera (plantain press), flatten the plantains. Fry the flattened plantains again for 2-3 minutes on each side, until they are crispy and golden brown. Remove from the skillet and sprinkle with salt to taste. Serve hot.

CERDO AL CURRY CON COCO (PORK CURRY WITH COCONUT)

Ingredients:

1 kg pork loin, cut into cubes
1 onion, chopped
3 garlic cloves, minced
2 tablespoons curry powder
1 can of coconut milk
1 tablespoon vegetable oil
Salt and pepper to taste

Instructions:

In a large pot or Dutch oven, heat the vegetable oil over medium-high heat. Add the pork cubes and cook until browned on all sides, about 5-7 minutes. Remove the pork from the pot and set aside. In the same pot, add the onion and garlic and cook until softened, about 3-4 minutes. Add the curry powder and cook for 1-2 minutes, stirring constantly. Add the coconut milk and bring to a simmer. Return the pork to the pot and stir to combine Cover and simmer over low heat for 1-2 hours or until the pork is tender. Season with salt and pepper to taste. Serve hot with rice.

ARROZ ATOLLADO DE CARNE AHUMADA (SMOKED MEAT RICE STEW)

Ingredients:

1 kg smoked beef or pork, shredded
2 cups rice
4 cups chicken or beef broth
2 tablespoons vegetable oil
1 onion, chopped
3 garlic cloves, minced
1 red bell pepper, chopped
1 green bell pepper, chopped
1 cup peas
1/2 cup chopped cilantro
Salt and pepper to taste

Instructions:

In a large pot or Dutch oven, heat the vegetable oil over medium-high heat. Add the onion, garlic, and bell peppers and cook until softened, about 3-4 minutes. Add the shredded smoked meat and cook for another 2-3 minutes, stirring occasionally. Add the rice and stir to coat with the vegetables and meat. Pour in the broth and bring to a boil. Reduce the heat to low, cover, and simmer for about 20-25 minutes, or until the rice is tender and the liquid is absorbed. Stir in the peas and cilantro and season with salt and pepper to taste. Serve hot.

MUCHACHO RELLENO COLOMBIANO

Ingredients:

2 lbs flank steak
1 onion, finely chopped
4 garlic cloves, minced
1/2 red bell pepper, chopped
1/2 green bell pepper, chopped
2 tablespoons of tomato paste
2 cups of beef broth
1/4 teaspoon ground cumin
1/4 teaspoon paprika
Salt and pepper to taste
2 hard boiled eggs, sliced
1/2 cup of raisins
1/2 cup of chopped green olives
Toothpicks

Instructions:

Preheat your oven to 350°F. Heat some oil in a skillet over medium heat. Add the onions, garlic, and peppers and cook until softened. Add the tomato paste, cumin, paprika, salt, and pepper, and stir until everything is combined. Add the beef broth and let the mixture simmer for about 10 minutes, or until it thickens. Pound the flank steak with a meat mallet until it's thin and even. Spread the filling over the steak, leaving about an inch around the edges. Place the sliced eggs, raisins, and olives over the filling. Carefully roll the steak up and secure it with toothpicks. Heat some oil in a pan over medium-high heat. Brown the steak on all sides. Transfer the steak to a baking dish and bake for about 45 minutes, or until the internal temperature reaches 145°F. Remove the steak from the oven and let it rest

CAMILA NAVIA

for a few minutes before slicing. Serve the sliced steak with the sauce from the pan.

Enjoy your Muchacho relleno colombiano!

LASAÑA DE ATÚN

Ingredients:

1 pound lasagna noodles
2 cans of tuna, drained and flaked
2 cups tomato sauce
1 cup ricotta cheese
1/2 cup grated Parmesan cheese
1/2 cup shredded mozzarella cheese
2 cloves garlic, minced
1/4 cup chopped fresh parsley
1/4 cup chopped fresh basil
Salt and pepper to taste
2 tablespoons olive oil

Instructions:

Preheat the oven to 375°F (190°C). Cook the lasagna noodles according to the package directions. Drain and set aside. In a large mixing bowl, combine the tuna, tomato sauce, ricotta cheese, Parmesan cheese, mozzarella cheese, garlic, parsley, basil, salt, and pepper. Mix well. Spread a thin layer of the tuna mixture over the bottom of a 9x13 inch baking dish. Top with a layer of lasagna noodles, followed by another layer of the tuna mixture. Repeat the layers until all of the ingredients are used up, ending with a layer of the tuna mixture. Drizzle the top with olive oil. Cover the baking dish with aluminum foil and bake for 30 minutes. Remove the foil and bake for an additional 10-15 minutes, or until the top is golden brown and the lasagna is heated through. Let the lasagna cool for a few minutes before slicing and serving.

ROLLO DE POLLO NAVIDEÑO

Ingredients:

2 boneless, skinless chicken breasts
1/4 cup chopped ham
1/4 cup chopped cooked bacon
1/4 cup chopped almonds
1/4 cup chopped prunes
1/4 cup chopped raisins
1/4 cup chopped olives
1/4 cup chopped green onions
1/4 cup chopped red bell pepper
1/4 cup chopped yellow bell pepper
2 tablespoons olive oil
Salt and pepper to taste

Instructions:

Preheat the oven to 375°F (190°C). Butterfly the chicken breasts and pound them to an even thickness. Season with salt and pepper. In a mixing bowl, combine the ham, bacon, almonds, prunes, raisins, olives, green onions, red bell pepper, yellow bell pepper, and olive oil. Mix well. Spread the mixture over the chicken breasts. Roll up the chicken breasts and tie them with kitchen twine to secure. Place the chicken breasts in a baking dish and bake for 30-35 minutes, or until the chicken is cooked through. Let the chicken rest for a few minutes before slicing and serving.

LENTEJAS CON CHORIZO

Ingredients:

1 pound (450g) dried lentils, rinsed and picked over
1 large onion, chopped
3 cloves garlic, minced
1 green bell pepper, chopped
2 carrots, chopped
2 chorizo sausages, sliced
1 can (14.5 ounces/400g) diced tomatoes
4 cups (960ml) chicken or vegetable broth
1 tablespoon olive oil
1 teaspoon smoked paprika
Salt and pepper, to taste
Fresh parsley, chopped (optional)

Instructions:

In a large pot, heat the olive oil over medium heat. Add the onion, garlic, green bell pepper, and carrots, and cook until the vegetables are tender, about 5-7 minutes. Add the sliced chorizo and cook for another 2-3 minutes, until the sausage is browned. Add the diced tomatoes, chicken or vegetable broth, and smoked paprika to the pot, and stir to combine. Bring to a boil, then reduce the heat and let simmer for 10 minutes. Add the lentils to the pot and stir to combine. Bring back to a boil, then reduce the heat and let simmer for 30-40 minutes, until the lentils are tender and the flavors have melded together. Season with salt and pepper to taste. Garnish with chopped fresh parsley, if desired. Serve hot with crusty bread, rice, or potatoes. Enjoy!

LENTEJAS CON VERDURAS

Ingredients:

1 cup of lentils, rinsed and drained
4 cups of water
1 onion, chopped
3 garlic cloves, minced
2 tomatoes, chopped
2 carrots, peeled and chopped
2 celery stalks, chopped
1 red bell pepper, chopped
1 teaspoon of ground cumin
1 teaspoon of smoked paprika
1 bay leaf
1 tablespoon of olive oil
Salt and pepper to taste

Instructions:

In a large pot, heat the olive oil over medium heat. Add the onion and garlic and cook until the onion is translucent. Add the tomatoes, carrots, celery, and red bell pepper to the pot and cook for a few minutes until the vegetables start to soften. Add the lentils, water, cumin, smoked paprika, bay leaf, salt, and pepper to the pot. Bring the mixture to a boil, then reduce the heat to low, cover the pot, and simmer for about 30-40 minutes until the lentils are tender. Serve the lentil soup hot, garnished with chopped parsley if desired.

TORTILLAS DE HUEVO CON ATÚN

Ingredients:

4 eggs
1 can of tuna, drained
1/4 onion, finely chopped
1/4 red bell pepper, finely chopped
Salt and pepper to taste
1 tablespoon of olive oil

Instructions:

In a mixing bowl, whisk together the eggs, tuna, onion, red bell pepper, salt, and pepper. In a non-stick skillet, heat the olive oil over medium heat. Pour the egg and tuna mixture into the skillet and cook for 3-4 minutes until the bottom is set. Use a spatula to flip the tortilla and cook the other side for another 2-3 minutes until cooked through. Cut the tortilla into wedges and serve hot or cold.

BUTIFARRA

Ingredients:

1 pound of ground pork
1/4 cup of red wine vinegar
1 tablespoon of paprika
1 teaspoon of cumin
1 teaspoon of salt
1/2 teaspoon of black pepper
1/2 teaspoon of dried oregano
1/4 teaspoon of red pepper flakes
2 garlic cloves, minced
1/4 onion, finely chopped
1/4 cup of bread crumbs
1 egg

Instructions:

In a mixing bowl, combine the ground pork, red wine vinegar, paprika, cumin, salt, black pepper, dried oregano, red pepper flakes, garlic, onion, bread crumbs, and egg. Mix the ingredients together until well combined. Form the mixture into sausage-shaped patties. Heat a non-stick skillet over medium-high heat and cook the butifarra for about 3-4 minutes per side, or until fully cooked. Serve the butifarra hot, garnished with chopped parsley or cilantro if desired.

SALMÓN CON PURÉ DE PAPA CRIOLLA

Ingredients:

4 salmon fillets
Salt and black pepper
2 tbsp olive oil
4 cups of criolla potatoes, peeled and cut into cubes
1/2 cup of heavy cream
1/4 cup of butter
1/4 cup of grated Parmesan cheese
Salt and black pepper to taste

Instructions:

Preheat the oven to 400°F (200°C). Season the salmon fillets with salt and black pepper and set them aside. Heat the olive oil in a large skillet over medium heat. Add the cubed potatoes and cook until they are soft and lightly browned, stirring occasionally. Transfer the cooked potatoes to a large bowl and add the heavy cream, butter, and Parmesan cheese. Mash the potatoes until they are smooth and creamy. Season with salt and black pepper to taste. Place the seasoned salmon fillets in a baking dish and bake in the preheated oven for 12-15 minutes, or until cooked through. Serve the salmon hot with a generous scoop of the mashed potato criolla on the side. Enjoy!

DRINKS AND BEVERAGES

COCTEL DE CAFÉ

Ingredients:

1 shot of espresso or strong coffee
1/2 cup of milk
1 tbsp of sugar
1/4 tsp of vanilla extract
Ice

Instructions:

In a blender, combine the espresso or coffee, milk, sugar, and vanilla extract. Add ice to the blender and blend until smooth and frothy. Pour the mixture into a glass and serve.

SALSA COCTEL

Ingredients:

1/2 cup of ketchup
1 tbsp of horseradish
1 tbsp of Worcestershire sauce
1/2 tsp of hot sauce
1 tbsp of lemon juice
Salt and pepper to taste

Instructions:

In a bowl, whisk together the ketchup, horseradish, Worcestershire sauce, hot sauce, lemon juice, salt, and pepper until well combined. Taste and adjust seasoning as needed. Cover and chill until ready to serve.

BATIDO DE MOCKA

Ingredients:

1 cup of brewed coffee, chilled
1/2 cup of milk
1 tbsp of sugar
1 tbsp of chocolate syrup
1/2 tsp of vanilla extract
Ice

Instructions:

In a blender, combine the coffee, milk, sugar, chocolate syrup, and vanilla extract. Add ice to the blender and blend until smooth and frothy. Pour the mixture into a glass and serve.

PONCHE TROPICAL

Ingredients:

2 cups of diced pineapple
2 cups of diced mango
2 cups of diced papaya
1 cup of orange juice
1 cup of pineapple juice
1 cup of coconut cream
1 cup of rum (optional)
Ice

Instructions:

In a blender, puree the diced pineapple, mango, and papaya until smooth. Add the orange juice, pineapple juice, and coconut cream and blend until combined. If desired, add rum to the blender and pulse a few times to incorporate. Pour the mixture over ice and serve.

AVENA

Ingredients:

1 cup of rolled oats
2 cups of water
1 cinnamon stick
1/2 teaspoon of salt
1 can of evaporated milk
1 can of sweetened condensed milk
Ground cinnamon (for garnish)

Instructions:

In a saucepan, combine the rolled oats, water, cinnamon stick, and salt. Bring to a boil over high heat. Reduce the heat to low and simmer, stirring occasionally, until the oats are tender and the mixture has thickened, about 20 minutes. Remove the cinnamon stick and discard. Stir in the evaporated milk and sweetened condensed milk until well combined. Divide the avena among individual serving bowls and sprinkle with ground cinnamon.

CASPIROLETA

Ingredients:

2 cups of water
1 cinnamon stick
3 cloves
1/2 cup of brown sugar
1/2 cup of grated panela (or brown sugar)
1/2 cup of diced queso blanco (or white cheese)
2 egg yolks
1/2 cup of brandy (optional)
Ground cinnamon (for garnish)

Instructions:

In a saucepan, combine the water, cinnamon stick, cloves, brown sugar, and grated panela. Bring to a boil over high heat. Reduce the heat to low and simmer, stirring occasionally, until the sugar has dissolved and the mixture has thickened slightly, about 10 minutes. Add the diced queso blanco and stir until melted and well combined. In a separate bowl, whisk the egg yolks until pale yellow and thick. Slowly pour a ladleful of the hot mixture into the egg yolks, whisking constantly to temper the eggs. Pour the egg mixture back into the saucepan and stir until well combined. If desired, add brandy to the saucepan and stir to combine. Ladle the caspiroleta into individual serving mugs and sprinkle with ground cinnamon.

CREMA DE CAFÉ COLOMBIANA

Ingredients:

4 cups of strong brewed coffee
2 cups of milk
1/4 cup of sugar
1 teaspoon of vanilla extract
Cinnamon sticks

Instructions:

In a large pot, combine the coffee, milk, sugar, and vanilla extract. Heat the mixture over medium heat until the sugar has dissolved and the mixture is hot, but not boiling. Remove from heat and serve hot in mugs, garnished with a cinnamon stick.

AGUA DE PANELA

Ingredients:

1 block of panela (solid unrefined cane sugar)
8 cups of water
Juice of 2 limes

Instructions:

In a medium-sized pot, heat the panela and water over medium heat.Stir occasionally until the panela has dissolved. Add the lime juice and stir. Let the mixture cool to room temperature, then strain it to remove any solids.Serve over ice and enjoy!

CHICHA

Ingredients:

2 cups of white rice
8 cups of water
1 cinnamon stick
1 cup of brown sugar
1 can of evaporated milk
1 teaspoon of vanilla extract
Ice cubes

Instructions:

Rinse the rice and put it in a large pot with the water and cinnamon stick. Bring to a boil. Reduce the heat and simmer for 45 minutes or until the rice is cooked. Remove from the heat and let cool. Strain the mixture through a fine sieve or cheesecloth. Add the brown sugar, evaporated milk, and vanilla extract to the strained mixture. Stir well and chill in the refrigerator. Serve over ice and enjoy!

MASATO

Ingredients:

2 cups of yuca (cassava) or corn flour
2 cups of water
1 cup of sugar
1 cinnamon stick
1 clove
1 orange peel
4 liters of water
1 tablespoon of chopped pineapple peel
1 tablespoon of chopped sweet potato peel

Instructions:

In a bowl, mix the yuca or corn flour with 2 cups of water and stir well until there are no lumps. In a pot, boil 4 liters of water with the cinnamon stick, clove, and orange peel. Once the water is boiling, add the mixture of yuca or corn flour and stir continuously until it thickens. Add the sugar and stir until it dissolves. Add the chopped pineapple peel and sweet potato peel and let it simmer for about 15 minutes. Remove from heat and let it cool. Strain the masato and serve chilled.

LA MACANA

Ingredients:

1 cup of panela (solid cane sugar)
2 cups of water
1 cinnamon stick
1 clove
1 star anise
1 orange peel
1 lime peel
1 lemon peel
1/2 cup of rum
1/2 cup of aguardiente (anise-flavored liquor)

Instructions:

In a pot, boil the panela with the water until it dissolves. Add the cinnamon stick, clove, star anise, orange peel, lime peel, and lemon peel. Let it simmer for about 30 minutes. Remove from heat and let it cool. Add the rum and aguardiente and mix well. Strain the la macana and serve over ice.

FRESCO DE AGUACATE

Ingredients:

1 ripe avocado, pitted and peeled
2 cups of water
1/2 cup of sugar
Juice of 1 lime
Ice cubes

Instructions:

In a blender, blend the avocado with 1 cup of water until smooth. In a pot, boil the remaining 1 cup of water with the sugar until it dissolves. Let it cool. Mix the avocado puree, sugar water, and lime juice in a pitcher. Serve over ice.

CHOCOLATE CON LECHE DE COCO (COCONUT MILK HOT CHOCOLATE)

Ingredients:

2 cups coconut milk
1 cup whole milk
1/2 cup semisweet chocolate chips
1/4 cup unsweetened cocoa powder
1/4 cup sugar
1 tsp vanilla extract
Whipped cream (optional)

Instructions:

In a saucepan, combine the coconut milk, whole milk, chocolate chips, cocoa powder, sugar, and vanilla extract. Heat the mixture over medium heat, stirring constantly, until the chocolate chips have melted and the mixture is smooth. Reduce the heat to low and continue to cook for 2-3 minutes, stirring occasionally, until the mixture is hot but not boiling. Serve the hot chocolate in mugs, topped with whipped cream if desired.

CAFÉ HELADO SORPRESA (SURPRISE ICED COFFEE)

Ingredients:

2 cups strong brewed coffee, cooled
1 cup milk
1/2 cup sweetened condensed milk
1/2 cup chocolate chips
Whipped cream (optional)

Instructions:

In a blender, combine the cooled coffee, milk, sweetened condensed milk, and chocolate chips. Blend the mixture on high speed until the chocolate chips are fully incorporated and the mixture is smooth. Pour the mixture into a pitcher and refrigerate for at least 2 hours, or until chilled. To serve, pour the iced coffee into glasses and top with whipped cream if desired.

CREMA DE CAFÉ Y CHOCOLATE (COFFEE AND CHOCOLATE CREAM)

Ingredients:

1 cup heavy cream
1/4 cup sugar
1/4 cup unsweetened cocoa powder
2 tbsp instant coffee powder
Whipped cream and chocolate shavings, for garnish (optional)

Instructions:

In a mixing bowl, beat the heavy cream, sugar, cocoa powder, and instant coffee powder until soft peaks form.
Spoon the mixture into serving dishes or glasses. Cover and refrigerate for at least 1 hour, or until chilled and set. Garnish with whipped cream and chocolate shavings if desired before serving.

BATIDO DE BANANO AL CAFÉ (BANANA AND COFFEE SMOOTHIE)

Ingredients:

1 ripe banana
1 cup of cold brewed coffee
1/2 cup of milk
1 tbsp honey (optional)
Ice

Instructions:

Peel the banana and cut it into small chunks.
Combine banana, coffee, milk, and honey in a blender.
Add a handful of ice cubes.
Blend until smooth.
Serve immediately.

YOGURT DE CHOCOLATE (CHOCOLATE YOGURT)

Ingredients:

2 cups of plain Greek yogurt
1/4 cup of cocoa powder
1/4 cup of honey
1 tsp vanilla extract

Instructions:

In a large bowl, whisk together the Greek yogurt, cocoa powder, honey, and vanilla extract until smooth. Cover the bowl with plastic wrap and chill in the refrigerator for at least 30 minutes. Serve cold as a snack or dessert.

SORBETE DE FRESA (STRAWBERRY SORBET)

Ingredients:

4 cups of frozen strawberries
1 cup of water
1 cup of sugar
1/4 cup of freshly squeezed lemon juice

Instructions:

In a small saucepan, combine water and sugar. Heat over medium heat until the sugar is dissolved. Remove from heat and let it cool. In a blender, puree the frozen strawberries until smooth. Add the cooled sugar syrup and lemon juice to the blender and blend until fully combined. Pour the mixture into a freezer-safe container and freeze for at least 4 hours or overnight. Serve the sorbet scooped into bowls or cones.

CREMA DE LIMÓN (LEMON CREAM):

Ingredients:

1 can of condensed milk
1 can of evaporated milk
1/2 cup of lemon juice
1 tablespoon of grated lemon zest

Instructions:

In a blender, mix the condensed milk, evaporated milk, lemon juice and lemon zest until smooth. Pour the mixture into a saucepan and heat over low heat for 10 minutes, stirring constantly. Once it thickens, remove it from heat and let it cool. Serve cold.

SORBETE DE CHOCOLATE Y CAFÉ (CHOCOLATE AND COFFEE SORBET)

Ingredients:

1 cup of sugar
1/2 cup of unsweetened cocoa powder
2 cups of strong brewed coffee
1 tablespoon of vanilla extract

Instructions:

In a saucepan, combine the sugar and cocoa powder. Add the coffee and vanilla extract and whisk until smooth. Heat the mixture over low heat, stirring constantly, until the sugar dissolves. Remove from heat and let it cool to room temperature. Pour the mixture into an ice cream maker and churn according to the manufacturer's instructions. Freeze for a few hours until firm.

CHOCOLATE CON LECHE DE COCOS (CHOCOLATE WITH COCONUT MILK)

Ingredients:

2 cups of coconut milk
1/2 cup of unsweetened cocoa powder
1/2 cup of sugar
1 tsp vanilla extract
1/4 tsp salt
2 cups of milk

Instructions:

In a saucepan, combine the coconut milk, cocoa powder, and sugar over medium heat. Whisk the ingredients together until the sugar has dissolved and the mixture is smooth. Add the vanilla extract and salt and continue to whisk. Slowly pour in the milk, whisking constantly until everything is well combined. Heat the mixture over medium heat, stirring occasionally, until it is hot but not boiling. Serve immediately and enjoy!

CARAJILLO SOUL

Ingredients:

1 shot of espresso
1/2 oz of brandy
1/2 oz of Kahlua
1/2 oz of Baileys Irish Cream
1 cinnamon stick

Instructions:

Brew a shot of espresso and pour it into a heatproof glass or mug. Add the brandy, Kahlua, and Baileys Irish Cream to the glass. Stir the ingredients together. Place a cinnamon stick in the glass as a garnish. Enjoy your delicious carajillo soul!

BOXEADOR

Ingredients:

2 oz of tequila
3/4 oz of lime juice
3/4 oz of strawberry syrup
1/4 oz of Aperol
1/4 oz of agave nectar
Club soda
Ice
Fresh strawberries for garnish

Instructions:

Fill a shaker with ice and add the tequila, lime juice, strawberry syrup, Aperol, and agave nectar. Shake the ingredients together until they are well combined. Fill a glass with ice and strain the mixture into the glass. Top the drink with club soda and garnish with fresh strawberries. Serve and enjoy your refreshing boxeador!

DESSERTS

ALFAJORES COLOMBIANOS

Ingredients:

2 cups all-purpose flour
1 cup cornstarch
1/4 teaspoon salt
1/2 teaspoon baking soda
1 tablespoon baking powder
1/2 cup unsalted butter, softened
1/2 cup granulated sugar
3 egg yolks
1 teaspoon vanilla extract
1 can of dulce de leche
Powdered sugar, for dusting

Instructions:

Preheat oven to 350°F (180°C). In a bowl, sift together flour, cornstarch, salt, baking soda and baking powder. In a separate bowl, cream the butter and sugar until light and fluffy. Add the egg yolks and vanilla extract and mix well. Add the dry ingredients to the butter mixture, stirring until a soft dough forms. Roll the dough out on a floured surface and use a round cookie cutter to cut out circles. Place the circles on a baking sheet lined with parchment paper. Bake for 12-15 minutes or until the cookies are lightly golden. Let cool completely. Spread a teaspoon of dulce de leche on the flat side of one cookie and top with another cookie. Dust with powdered sugar and serve.

BUÑUELOS

Ingredients:

1 lb (500g) of yuca or cassava, peeled and grated
1/2 cup (60g) of cornstarch
1/2 teaspoon of baking powder
1 egg
1 tablespoon of sugar
1/4 teaspoon of salt
1/2 cup (120ml) of milk
1/4 cup (60ml) of vegetable oil
Powdered sugar, for dusting

Instructions:

In a large bowl, mix together the grated yuca, cornstarch, baking powder, egg, sugar, salt, and milk until a sticky dough forms. Heat the oil in a deep skillet over medium-high heat. Using a small ice cream scoop or spoon, form the dough into small balls. Carefully drop the balls into the hot oil and fry until golden brown, turning occasionally. Remove with a slotted spoon and drain on paper towels. Dust with powdered sugar and serve.

PASTEL DE COCO

Ingredients:

2 cups of grated coconut
1 can of sweetened condensed milk
3 egg yolks
1 tablespoon of cornstarch
1/2 cup of water
1/4 cup of sugar
1/4 teaspoon of salt
1/4 teaspoon of vanilla extract
1 pie crust

Instructions:

Preheat oven to 350°F (180°C). In a bowl, mix the coconut, condensed milk, and egg yolks until well combined.
Pour the mixture into the pie crust and smooth out the top. Bake for 25-30 minutes or until the filling is set. In a saucepan, whisk together the cornstarch, water, sugar, salt, and vanilla extract. Cook over medium heat, stirring constantly, until the mixture thickens and starts to boil.
Remove from heat and let cool for a few minutes. Pour the glaze over the pie and let cool completely before serving.

MANTECADA

Ingredients:

1 cup all-purpose flour
1/2 cup unsalted butter, at room temperature
1/2 cup granulated sugar
3 eggs, at room temperature
1/4 cup milk
1 teaspoon vanilla extract
1 teaspoon baking powder
Pinch of salt

Instructions:

Preheat the oven to 350°F (180°C). In a bowl, sift together the flour, baking powder, and salt. In a separate bowl, cream the butter and sugar together until light and fluffy. Add the eggs one at a time, beating well after each addition. Stir in the milk and vanilla extract. Gradually mix in the flour mixture, stirring until just combined. Pour the batter into a greased muffin tin, filling each cup about 2/3 full. Bake for 15-20 minutes, or until golden brown. Remove from the oven and let cool for a few minutes before removing from the tin. Serve warm or at room temperature.

FLAN DE CAFÉ
(COFFEE FLAN)

Ingredients:

1 can (14 oz) sweetened condensed milk
1 can (12 oz) evaporated milk
3 eggs
1/2 cup strong brewed coffee
1 teaspoon vanilla extract
1/2 cup granulated sugar

Instructions:

Preheat oven to 350°F. In a large mixing bowl, whisk together sweetened condensed milk, evaporated milk, eggs, coffee, and vanilla extract until smooth. In a medium saucepan, heat granulated sugar over medium heat, stirring constantly, until melted and golden brown.
Pour melted sugar into a 9-inch round cake pan, swirling to coat the bottom evenly. Pour flan mixture into the cake pan over the caramelized sugar. Place cake pan in a larger baking dish and fill the larger dish with hot water until it reaches halfway up the sides of the cake pan. Bake for 45-50 minutes, or until the flan is set and a toothpick inserted into the center comes out clean. Remove from oven and let cool to room temperature. Once cooled, refrigerate for at least 2 hours or overnight. To serve, run a knife around the edge of the cake pan to loosen the flan, then invert onto a serving plate. The caramel sauce will drizzle over the top of the flan.

POSTRE BORRACHO (DRUNKEN DESSERT):

Ingredients:

1 pound of cake (pound cake, sponge cake, or similar), sliced
1/2 cup of rum
1 can of condensed milk
1 can of evaporated milk
1 cup of whipped cream
1/2 teaspoon of cinnamon

Instructions:

In a mixing bowl, whisk together the condensed milk, evaporated milk, whipped cream, and cinnamon until smooth. Add the rum and stir to combine. Place a layer of cake slices in a serving dish or individual dessert cups. Pour some of the milk mixture over the cake layer, using enough to moisten the cake but not make it soggy. Repeat layering with cake slices and milk mixture until all of the ingredients are used up. Cover the dish or cups with plastic wrap and refrigerate for at least 2 hours, or until the milk mixture has been absorbed by the cake. Serve chilled.

BANANOS CALADOS

Ingredients:

4 ripe bananas, peeled and sliced
1/2 cup of grated panela
1 cinnamon stick
1 1/2 cups of water

Instructions:

In a medium saucepan, mix the water, panela, and cinnamon stick over medium heat until the panela is dissolved. Add the banana slices to the saucepan and let it cook for about 10-15 minutes or until the bananas are soft and the syrup has thickened. Remove from heat and let it cool for a few minutes before serving. Serve the bananas with the syrup, and you can also add a dollop of whipped cream or a sprinkle of cinnamon on top, if desired. Enjoy your delicious bananos calados!

DULCE DE COCO

Ingredients:

2 cups shredded coconut
1 1/2 cups brown sugar
1/2 cup water
1 cinnamon stick

Instructions:

In a saucepan, combine the shredded coconut, brown sugar, water, and cinnamon stick. Cook over medium heat, stirring constantly, until the sugar dissolves and the mixture thickens. Reduce the heat to low and continue stirring until the mixture starts to come away from the sides of the pan, about 15-20 minutes. Remove from heat and let it cool down for a few minutes. With the help of a spoon, shape small portions of the mixture into balls or cylinders.

FLAN DE QUESO

Ingredients:

1 can (14 oz) sweetened condensed milk
1 can (12 oz) evaporated milk
4 eggs
1 teaspoon vanilla extract
1/2 cup sugar
1/2 cup water
1 cup cream cheese, at room temperature

Instructions:

Preheat the oven to 350°F. In a saucepan, combine the sugar and water over medium heat. Cook, stirring occasionally, until the sugar has dissolved and the mixture has thickened slightly. Pour the sugar mixture into a 9-inch round baking dish, tilting the dish to coat the bottom and sides evenly. In a blender, combine the sweetened condensed milk, evaporated milk, eggs, vanilla extract, and cream cheese. Blend until smooth. Pour the mixture into the prepared baking dish. Place the baking dish in a large roasting pan and fill the pan with enough hot water to come halfway up the sides of the baking dish. Bake for 50-60 minutes, or until a toothpick inserted in the center comes out clean. Remove the flan from the oven and let it cool to room temperature. Chill the flan in the refrigerator for at least 2 hours before serving.

ARROZ CON LECHE

Ingredients:

1 cup rice
1 can (14 oz) sweetened condensed milk
1 can (12 oz) evaporated milk
2 cinnamon sticks
4 cups water
1/4 cup raisins (optional)

Instructions:

In a large saucepan, combine the rice, water, and cinnamon sticks. Bring to a boil over high heat, then reduce the heat to low, cover, and simmer for 15 minutes. Add the sweetened condensed milk, evaporated milk, and raisins (if using) to the pot. Stir well to combine. Continue to simmer over low heat, uncovered, stirring occasionally, for another 30-40 minutes, or until the mixture has thickened and the rice is fully cooked.

Remove the cinnamon sticks and let the rice pudding cool down to room temperature. Chill the rice pudding in the refrigerator for at least 1 hour before serving.

MIELMESABE

Ingredients:

1 cup grated coconut
1 cup sugar
1 cup water
1/4 teaspoon cinnamon

Instructions:

In a saucepan, combine the grated coconut, sugar, water, and cinnamon. Cook over medium heat, stirring constantly, until the mixture thickens and the coconut is cooked, about 20-25 minutes. Remove from heat and allow to cool. The mielmesabe can be served warm or cold, as a topping for fruits or desserts, or on its own.

FLAN DE MANGO

Ingredients:

1 can sweetened condensed milk
1 can evaporated milk
1 cup mango puree
4 eggs
1 teaspoon vanilla extract
1/2 cup sugar
1/4 cup water

Instructions:

Preheat the oven to 350°F (180°C). In a saucepan, heat the sugar and water over medium heat, stirring constantly, until the sugar dissolves and the mixture turns into a caramel. Pour the caramel into a 9-inch flan mold, swirling it around to coat the bottom and sides. Set aside.
In a blender, combine the condensed milk, evaporated milk, mango puree, eggs, and vanilla extract. Blend until smooth. Pour the mixture into the caramel-coated flan mold. Cover with aluminum foil and place in a baking dish. Pour hot water into the baking dish to come halfway up the sides of the flan mold. Bake for 1 hour or until set. Remove from the oven and let cool. Refrigerate for at least 2 hours or overnight. To serve, run a knife around the edges of the flan and invert onto a serving platter. The caramel will form a sauce around the flan.

NATILLA

Ingredients:

4 cups whole milk
1/2 cup cornstarch
1/2 cup sugar
2 cinnamon sticks
2 cloves
1/2 teaspoon ground nutmeg
1 teaspoon vanilla extract

Instructions:

In a large saucepan, combine the milk, cornstarch, sugar, cinnamon sticks, cloves, and nutmeg. Whisk until smooth. Cook over medium heat, stirring constantly, until the mixture thickens and comes to a boil, about 10-15 minutes. Remove from heat and stir in the vanilla extract. Remove the cinnamon sticks and cloves. Pour the mixture into a serving dish or individual bowls. Let cool to room temperature, then refrigerate for at least 1 hour or until set. To serve, sprinkle ground cinnamon on top of the natilla.

TRUFAS AL CAFÉ (COFFEE TRUFFLES)

Ingredients:

250g of dark chocolate
1/2 cup of heavy cream
2 tablespoons of coffee liqueur
1 tablespoon of instant coffee
Cocoa powder for dusting

Instructions:

In a double boiler or a heatproof bowl set over a pot of simmering water, melt the chocolate and heavy cream together. Remove from heat and stir in the coffee liqueur and instant coffee until well combined. Let the mixture cool to room temperature, then cover and refrigerate for at least 2 hours, until firm. Line a baking sheet with parchment paper. Using a small cookie scoop or spoon, scoop out the chocolate mixture and roll into 1-inch balls. Roll each ball in cocoa powder until fully coated. Place the truffles on the prepared baking sheet and refrigerate until firm, about 30 minutes.Serve chilled.
Enjoy your delicious coffee truffles!

CREPES AL CAFÉ (COFFEE CREPES)

Ingredients:

1 cup all-purpose flour
1/2 cup milk
1/2 cup strong brewed coffee
2 eggs
2 tablespoons sugar
2 tablespoons butter, melted
1/2 teaspoon vanilla extract
Pinch of salt

Instructions:

In a mixing bowl, combine all the ingredients and whisk until smooth. Heat a non-stick skillet or crepe pan over medium-high heat. Pour 1/4 cup of the batter into the skillet and swirl to spread the batter evenly. Cook for about 1 minute or until the edges start to lift. Flip the crepe and cook for another 30 seconds. Repeat until all the batter is used up. Serve with whipped cream or your favorite filling.

PASTEL DE CAFÉ (COFFEE CAKE)

Ingredients:

2 cups all-purpose flour
1 cup granulated sugar
1 cup strong brewed coffee
1/2 cup vegetable oil
2 eggs
1 tablespoon baking powder
1 teaspoon vanilla extract
Pinch of salt

Instructions:

Preheat oven to 350°F (175°C). In a mixing bowl, combine all the ingredients and whisk until smooth. Pour the batter into a greased 9-inch (23cm) cake pan. Bake for 35-40 minutes or until a toothpick inserted in the center comes out clean. Let the cake cool before slicing and serving.

BANANOS CARAMELIZADOS CON HELADO DE VAINILLA

Ingredients:

4 ripe bananas, sliced
1/2 cup brown sugar
1/4 cup butter
1/4 cup rum (optional)
1 teaspoon vanilla extract
Pinch of salt
Vanilla ice cream

Instructions:

In a skillet, melt the butter and brown sugar over medium heat. Add the sliced bananas and cook for about 3-4 minutes or until softened. Add the rum (optional), vanilla extract, and salt. Cook for an additional 1-2 minutes. Serve the bananas warm with a scoop of vanilla ice cream on top.

COCADAS BUENAVENTURA

Ingredients:

2 cups grated coconut
1 can (14 oz) sweetened condensed milk
1/2 teaspoon vanilla extract
1/4 teaspoon salt
2 egg whites

Instructions:

Preheat oven to 350°F (175°C). In a mixing bowl, combine grated coconut, sweetened condensed milk, vanilla extract, and salt. Mix well. In another bowl, beat egg whites until stiff peaks form. Fold egg whites into the coconut mixture until well combined. Drop spoonfuls of the mixture onto a baking sheet lined with parchment paper. Bake for 15-20 minutes or until golden brown. Remove from the oven and let cool completely.

MOUSSE DE CHOCOLATE BLANCO (WHITE CHOCOLATE MOUSSE)

Ingredients:

7 oz white chocolate, chopped
3 tablespoons milk
2 teaspoons unflavored gelatin
1/4 cup cold water
1 cup heavy cream
2 egg whites
1/4 cup sugar

Instructions:

In a small saucepan, melt the white chocolate and milk over low heat. Set aside to cool. In another saucepan, sprinkle the gelatin over the cold water and let it sit for 5 minutes. Heat the gelatin mixture over low heat, stirring constantly, until the gelatin is completely dissolved. Remove from heat and stir in the melted white chocolate mixture. In a mixing bowl, whip the heavy cream until stiff peaks form. In another mixing bowl, beat the egg whites until soft peaks form. Gradually add sugar and continue beating until stiff peaks form. Gently fold the whipped cream and egg whites into the chocolate mixture until well combined. Divide the mixture into serving glasses and refrigerate for at least 2 hours or until set.

PANNA COTTA DE LIMONARIA (LEMON VERBENA PANNA COTTA)

Ingredients:

2 cups heavy cream
1/4 cup sugar
1 tablespoon lemon verbena leaves
2 teaspoons unflavored gelatin
1/4 cup cold water

Instructions:

In a saucepan, combine the heavy cream, sugar, and lemon verbena leaves. Heat over low heat until the sugar dissolves.

Remove from heat and let the mixture steep for 10 minutes. In another saucepan, sprinkle the gelatin over the cold water and let it sit for 5 minutes. Heat the gelatin mixture over low heat, stirring constantly, until the gelatin is completely dissolved. Strain the cream mixture through a fine-mesh sieve into a mixing bowl. Add the gelatin mixture to the cream mixture and stir well. Divide the mixture into serving glasses and refrigerate for at least 2 hours or until set. Serve chilled.

TORTA DE AUYAMA CON NIBS DE CACAO (PUMPKIN CAKE WITH CACAO NIBS)

Ingredients:

2 cups of grated pumpkin (auyama)
1/2 cup of unsalted butter
1 cup of brown sugar
3 eggs
1 1/2 cups of all-purpose flour
1 tsp of baking powder
1 tsp of cinnamon
1/2 tsp of ground ginger
1/4 tsp of ground nutmeg
1/4 tsp of salt
1/2 cup of milk
1/2 cup of cacao nibs

Instructions:

Preheat the oven to 350°F (180°C). Grease a 9-inch (23 cm) cake pan. In a large mixing bowl, cream the butter and sugar until light and fluffy. Add the eggs one at a time, beating well after each addition. In a separate bowl, whisk together the flour, baking powder, cinnamon, ginger, nutmeg, and salt. Add the dry ingredients to the creamed mixture alternately with the milk, beginning and ending with the dry ingredients. Beat well after each addition. Fold in the grated pumpkin and cacao nibs. Pour the batter into the prepared pan and smooth the top. Bake for 35-40 minutes or until a toothpick inserted into the center comes out clean. Cool the cake in the pan for 5 minutes, then transfer to a wire rack to cool completely.

PAN DE ESPONJA (SPONGE BREAD)

Ingredients:

1 lb (450 g) of all-purpose flour
1/2 oz (14 g) of active dry yeast
2 cups of lukewarm water
2 tsp of salt

Instructions:

In a large mixing bowl, combine the flour, yeast, and salt.
Add the water and mix until a smooth dough forms. Knead the dough on a floured surface for 10-15 minutes until it becomes elastic. Place the dough in a greased bowl, cover with a damp cloth, and let it rise in a warm place for 1-2 hours. Punch down the dough and divide it into 2-3 equal pieces. Shape each piece into a loaf and place them in greased bread pans. Let the loaves rise for another 30-60 minutes. Preheat the oven to 400°F (200°C). Bake the bread for 25-30 minutes or until golden brown. Cool the bread on a wire rack before slicing and serving.

PIONONOS

Ingredients:

4 ripe plantains
1/2 lb. ground beef
1/2 onion, finely chopped
1/2 red pepper, finely chopped
1 garlic clove, minced
1 tsp. ground cumin
Salt and pepper, to taste
Oil for frying

Instructions:

Peel the plantains and cut them into 1/2-inch thick slices. Heat the oil in a frying pan over medium heat. Fry the plantains for 3-4 minutes on each side, until they are golden brown. Remove the plantains from the pan and place them on a paper towel to drain. In a separate pan, cook the ground beef, onion, red pepper, garlic, cumin, salt, and pepper over medium-high heat, stirring frequently, until the beef is browned and cooked through. Preheat your oven to 375°F (190°C). On a baking sheet, lay out the plantains in a single layer. Using a spoon, place a small amount of the beef mixture on top of each plantain slice. Carefully roll up each plantain slice, securing it with a toothpick if necessary. Bake the piononos in the preheated oven for 10-15 minutes, until they are heated through and lightly browned. Serve hot.

MERENGÓN

Ingredients:

6 egg whites
1 1/2 cups sugar
1 tsp. white vinegar
1 tsp. vanilla extract
2 cups chopped fruit (such as strawberries, bananas, and pineapple)
1 cup heavy cream, whipped

Instructions:

Preheat your oven to 350°F (175°C). Line a baking sheet with parchment paper. In a large mixing bowl, beat the egg whites with an electric mixer until stiff peaks form. Gradually add the sugar, vinegar, and vanilla extract, continuing to beat until the mixture is glossy and forms stiff peaks. Spoon the meringue mixture onto the prepared baking sheet, forming a circle about 9 inches in diameter. Bake the meringue in the preheated oven for 10-12 minutes, until it is lightly browned and crisp on the outside but still soft on the inside. Allow the meringue to cool completely. Spread the chopped fruit over the top of the meringue. Spoon the whipped cream on top of the fruit. Serve immediately.

Printed in Great Britain
by Amazon

25751883R00115